Changing Times, Changing Worlds

やさしく読める社会事情

Joan McConnell   Kiyoshi Yamauchi

S **SEIBIDO**

photographs by

iStockphoto

音声ファイルのダウンロード／ストリーミング

CD マーク表示がある箇所は、音声を弊社 HP より無料でダウンロード／ストリーミングすることができます。トップページのバナーをクリックし、書籍検索してください。書籍詳細ページに音声ダウンロードアイコンがございますのでそちらから自習用音声としてご活用ください。

https://www.seibido.co.jp

Changing Times, Changing Worlds

PREFACE

Dear Students,

A textbook is a very special kind of book. Students spend weeks, often months, reading the passages, answering the questions, and listening to the CD recordings. That's why a textbook author must select topics that are informative, interesting and, at times, entertaining. After all, nobody likes a dull, dreary textbook!

Changing Times, *Changing Worlds* is a textbook about the changes taking place in our world today – changes in our values, our behavior, our relationships, our language and even our planet. Professor Yamauchi and I want you to learn about these changes, think about them, and – most of all – express your opinion about them.

This textbook has 15 chapters – 14 of which deal with specific topics about change. The final chapter is my Special Message to all my readers.

Each chapter has seven sections where you can practice reading, writing, listening and speaking – all in English!

In the first section, you will find introductory notes and *Pre-Reading Questions*. Then you are ready for the *Reading Passage* in section two. Professor Yamauchi has prepared helpful notes in Japanese.

In section three, you will answer the *Comprehension Questions*. Then you will complete the *Guided Summary* in section four. In section five, you will review *Essential Grammar*, and then do the Grammar Practice that Professor Yamauchi has prepared.

Section six is your "fun time." Please enjoy the lively *Dialogue* in "real-life" American English as well as the entertaining passage in Japanese about things you did not know!

Now It's Your Turn is the final section. Choose one of the three topics, and discuss it with your partner(s). Professor Yamauchi and I have included some sample answers as well as helpful hints.

I hope that you find *Changing Times*, *Changing Worlds* informative, interesting, and entertaining. If so, it will help you expand your understanding of the world and, at the same time, improve your English skills.

All my best wishes to you from sunny Florida,

Dr. Joanie McConnell

多くの優良テキストの中から、本書をお選びいただき誠にありがとうございます。

このテキストを英語学習の良き友としてご活用いただければ、やさしい語彙で書かれてはいながらも、非常にこなれた英文を読みながら、英文法の基礎を復習し、練習問題を通じ総合的な英語力を伸ばしつつ、大学生としてふさわしい社会問題について学び、さらに自分の意見を英語で述べることができる力をつけていただけるものと確信いたします。練習問題には様々な工夫を凝らし、皆様の学習効率が高まるよう配慮しました。

皆様の心の糧、そして知識の礎となるエッセイで全章を構成いたしましたので、きっとご満足いただけることと確信しております。

以下に挙げたねらいや目標を、頭にしっかり入れて学習なされば、学習効果が上がります。

1 Pre-Reading Questions

本文に出てくる語句の意味を確認しておくための練習問題です。これらの語句の意味をしっかりと確認して本文を読んでください。

2 Reading Passage（本文）

250 語前後でまとめられた平易な名文です。英文を読む楽しさを味わってください。音読もお勧めします。

● Notes

本文中に出てくる語句の解説です。英文を読む際の参考にしてください。英文を読むときに役立つ文化情報なども入れています。

3 Comprehension Questions

本文を読んだ直後に、その内容をどの程度理解できたかをチェックできます。

4 Guided Summary

本文の内容が簡潔に要約されています。活用法をご自分で考えてみましょう。
英文を要約する練習の解答例としても活用できます。

5 Essential Grammar

各章の本文で使用された文法事項について、まとめて説明をしています。高校時代までに習ったはずの文法事項だと思いますが、再確認してみましょう。英文法は、英語を理解し使用するための基礎です。英文法の基礎がしっかりしていれば、その上に頑丈でしっかりした建物を建てることができるのです。

• Grammar Practice

日本語訳を参考に、与えられた語句を並べ替えて正しい英文を作る問題です。チャプターで習う文法事項に関連した問題ですので、Essential Grammar の説明を参考に解いてみましょう。しっかりとできるまで何度でも挑戦してみましょう。全て正解できるようになったら、語群を隠して和文英訳問題としても挑戦してみてください。

6 Dialogue

会話問題です。本文のテーマに関する日本人話者とネイティブスピーカーとの会話となっています。覚えておけば会話で使えるフレーズを中心に空欄にしていますので、音声を聞き、書き取ってください。また、実際に会話をしているつもりで練習をしてみましょう。チャプターのトピックについて英語で話す時の参考にしてください。

• コラム Did You Know?

本文の内容に関連したコラムを書いています。英語学習で疲れた頭を休めながら読んでください。気楽に読みながらも新しい知識も身に着けてもらえるような内容になっています。

7 Now It's Your Turn!

文字通り「さあ、あなたの番です！」。各章で述べられている社会問題について、あなたの考えを英語で述べる練習をする問題です。留学や仕事などで英語を使う場合、自分の意見をその理由ともに表現できることは極めて重要なことです。ペア練習などで他人の意見を聞く練習もしてください。

CONTENTS

Chapter 1

Smokey Bear:
A Mascot with a Message

日本にもいろいろなマスコットがいます。最近は、各自治体の「ゆるキャラ」が作られ、そのコンテスト（グランプリ）なども行われています。

　本章では、アメリカ人なら誰もが知っている山火事防止のマスコット、スモーキー・ベア（Smokey Bear）について学びましょう。

① Pre-Reading Questions 2

以下のイラストを参考にして、英文の下線部の意味を枠内の選択肢より選んで記号（a～f）で答えましょう。

| 1 famous | 2 rescue | 3 dangers |
| 4 firefighters | 5 discussion | 6 plane |

1. Toyotomi Hideyoshi was a <u>famous</u> samurai.　　　　　　　　　[　]
2. My uncle <u>rescued</u> the baby bear.　　　　　　　　　　　　　　[　]
3. It's important to understand the <u>dangers</u> of wildfires.　　　　[　]
4. <u>Firefighters</u> protect people, property and nature from fires.　[　]
5. In a <u>discussion</u>, you can talk about a problem, and hopefully find a
solution.　　　　　　　　　　　　　　　　　　　　　　　　　　　[　]
6. Travel by <u>plane</u> is safer than travel by car.　　　　　　　　　[　]

| a) 飛行機 | b) 危険 | c) 消防士 |
| d) 議論 | e) 有名な | f) 救助する |

Smokey Bear: A Mascot with a Message　**1**

PREVENT
WILDFIRES

Smokey Bear is probably the most famous American mascot. For more than 75 years, he has been reminding Americans about the dangers of wildfires.

Smokey Bear's story began in 1944. Because of the war, there were very
5 few firefighters. For this reason, the US Forest Service wanted the American public to learn about fire prevention. They needed a mascot to send this message.

After much discussion, Smokey Bear became their mascot. He looked so friendly and cute in his overalls and forest ranger's hat. His message was
10 direct: *Only you can prevent forest fires!*

Smokey Bear was a huge success because people loved him and, more important, paid attention to his message. But a real-life Smokey Bear made the mascot even more famous. Who was this bear?

In 1950, a huge wildfire broke out in the mountains of New Mexico.
15 Although the damage to the forests and wildlife was enormous, the firefighters rescued a badly burned baby bear. They called him Smokey Bear in honor of the famous mascot.

After a full recovery, Smokey Bear was flown by private plane to the National Zoo in Washington, D.C. There he had millions of visitors. People
20 wrote him letters, while some even sent him jars of honey.

Unfortunately he died in 1976, but the mascot Smokey Bear is still "alive." His message never changes. When you prevent wildfires, you protect nature and wildlife. Don't you agree that mascots are powerful tools for sending important messages?

(Words: 243)

Notes

wildfire(s): 山火事 (米国内で発生する山火事の 90% が人災である)
the US Forest Service: 米国林野局
Smokey Bear: スモーキー・ベア (スモーキーというニックネームの消防士にちなんで名づけられた)
forest ranger's hat: 森林レンジャー用帽子 (スモーキー・ベア・ハットとして知られている)

real-life Smokey Bear: 実在のスモーキー・ベア
wrote him letters: 手紙を書いた (Smokey Bear 用の郵便番号 〈20252〉もある)
jar(s) of honey: ハチミツのつぼ
prevent: 予防する、防ぐ

③ Comprehension Questions

本文の内容に合っている文には T を、合っていない文には F を [   ] に記入しましょう。

1. The US Forest Service chose Smokey Bear as their mascot because they wanted to teach Americans how to prevent wildfires. [   ]
2. In 1950, firefighters rescued a baby bear from a terrible wildfire, and named him Smokey Bear. [   ]
3. When the real-life Smokey Bear died, so did the mascot. [   ]
4. Preventing wildfires helps protect nature and wildlife. [   ]

④ Guided Summary 🎧 CD 4

次の英文は本文を要約したものです。(1) から (8) の空所に、下の (a) ～ (h) から適語を選んで記入し文を完成させましょう。

In 1944, the US Forest Service wanted Americans to learn more about fire (1)_____. They named their (2)_____ Smokey Bear. Everybody loved this cute mascot. Smokey Bear became even more popular after (3)_____ rescued a baby bear that was burned in a (4)_____. They named him Smokey Bear in honor of their mascot. After his (5)_____, Smokey Bear was flown by private plane to the National Zoo in Washington, D.C. He had millions of (6)_____. He died in 1976, but the mascot Smokey Bear is still "alive." He reminds us that preventing wildfires (7)_____ nature and (8)_____.

🔊 Word List

(a) wildfire	(b) protects	(c) mascot	(d) recovery
(e) prevention	(f) wildlife	(g) firefighters	(h) visitors

5 Essential Grammar　接続詞

文中の語と語、句と句、または、節と節を結びつける語を接続詞といいます。接続詞には等位接続詞と従位接続詞があります。

等位接続詞

接続詞の前後の節 [語・句] が対等の関係になるもので、and, but, so, or, nor, for などがあります。

ex 1）Unfortunately he died in 1976, but the mascot Smokey Bear is still "alive."
（本文第 7 段落）

ex 2）Boys went outdoors, and girls stayed indoors. (男子は屋外に行った、そして女子は室内にとどまった)

従位接続詞

従位接続詞は、節と節を結びつける働きをし、従位接続詞によって導かれる節を従属節、文の中心になる節を主節といいます。

1)　副詞節を導く接続詞

時、原因・理由、譲歩などを表す副詞節を導きます。

ex 3）When you prevent wildfires, you protect nature and wildlife. (本文第 7 段落)

ex 4）Although the damage to the forests and wildlife was enormous, the firefighters rescued a badly burned baby bear. (本文第 5 段落)

2)　名詞節を導く接続詞

ex 5）Don't you agree that mascots are powerful tools for sending important messages? (本文第 7 段落)

Grammar Practice

次の日本語文に合うように英語文を完成させましょう。ただし文頭に来る語も小文字にしてあります。

1. 人々はスモーキー・ベアを愛していましたが、彼は 1976 年に亡くなりました。

[Smokey Bear, / but / in 1976 / he / loved / died / people].

_____

2. あなたがリサイクルをする時、あなたは自然環境を守ることになります。

[the / recycle / you / natural environment / when / you / protect].

_____

3. 損害は甚大でしたが、彼らは一頭の赤ちゃんのクマを救いました。

[the damage / a baby bear / although / was / rescued / enormous, / they].

_____

4. あなたはそれが有名なマスコットであることに同意しますか？

[that / agree / it / you / do / a famous mascot / is]?

_____

6 Dialogue 🎧 5

音声を聞いて、日本語を参考にしながら空欄に聞き取った英語を書きましょう。

Yoko is talking to her friend Steve, an exchange student from California, about the terrible wildfires in California.

Yoko: Steve, you're from California, aren't you? So you must be really worried about all the wildfires there.

Steve: I sure am! I mean, it's a real disaster. These fires have destroyed forests, wildlife and people's homes.

Yoko: Just so sad! And lots of people have died or been injured.
_____ to stop these fires.
　　　　　　（ 何かしなければ ）

Steve: _____! Unfortunately humans cause so
　　　　　（ 言うは易し、行うは難し ）
many of these fires because they are too careless.

Yoko: Yeah, but what about climate change?   Isn't that something we have to think about?

Steve: That's a really serious problem. Recently we've had less rain and stronger storms, so more wildfires.

Yoko: _____, or things will get worse.
　　　　　（ 私たちが解決法を見つけなければ ）

Notes | **disaster:** 災害　　**climate change:** 気候変動　　**storm(s):** 嵐

🌐 Did You Know?

ワシントン DC の国立動物園内のスモーキー・ベアはとてもたくさんの手紙を受け取りました。そこで、合衆国郵便公社は彼に専用の郵便番号 20252 を与えました。人々は、彼に手紙やおもちゃや、さらに壺入りのハチミツまでも送りました。彼が 1976 年に亡くなった時、彼の亡骸は故郷のニューメキシコ州の山に飛行機で運ばれました。今日でも、世界中の人々がスモーキー・ベア歴史公園の彼の墓を参拝しています。

7 Now It's Your Turn!

次の３つのトピックから１つ選び、回答例や Useful Expressions を参考にしながらパートナーと話し合ってみましょう。準備として、自分の意見をまとめておくと話し合いやすくなります。

1. Do you think that mascots such as Smokey Bear can send powerful messages?

2. Wildfires are destroying nature, wildlife and property in many countries. What can we do to solve this problem?

3. Do you think that there are too many mascots in Japan and that some of them should be eliminated?

番号：☐

自分の意見 ....
....
....

回答例

1. Yes, I think that mascots like Smokey Bear really send powerful messages. Mascots are cute and fun, so people pay attention. Messages from humans can be boring.

2. We have to educate people about fire prevention. Too many wildfires are caused by humans – campfires, cigarettes and unfortunately arson.

3. Definitely! There are too many mascots, so I always get confused. And tourists don't understand them!

Useful Expressions

- I think messages from mascots are ...: マスコットキャラクターのメッセージは〜だと思います。
- We have to educate people about ...: 〜について私たちは人々を教育しなければなりません。
- There are too many mascots, so I always get confused. マスコットキャラクターがあまりにも多いので、私はいつも混乱します。
- Many mascots promote tourism, and teach us about local cultures.: 多くのマスコットキャラクターが観光を促し、地域文化を教えてくれます。

Chapter 2

Overtourism is a Problem!

本章のテーマは"overtourism"ですが、この語はまだ多くの辞書には掲載されていません。訳語はとりあえず「オーバーツーリズム」としています。簡単に説明すると「旅行者が多すぎる状態」のことです。本文中には日本の例は出ていませんが、一例を挙げると秋の観光シーズンの京都など、宿泊先の確保も難しい状態になっています。

1 Pre-Reading Questions 6

以下のイラストを参考にして、英文の下線部の意味を枠内の選択肢より選んで記号（a～f）で答えましょう。

1 works of art	2 variety	3 souvenirs
4 public transportation	5 tourists	6 discount tours

1. In Italy, you can see many beautiful <u>works of art</u>. [　　]
2. In France, you can taste a <u>variety</u> of delicious local specialties. [　　]
3. <u>Souvenirs</u> remind you of the places you visited. [　　]
4. Japan has an excellent system of <u>public transportation</u>. [　　]
5. During the summer, there are too many <u>tourists</u> in Europe. [　　]
6. To save money, many people go on <u>discount tours</u> during off-season.
   [　　]

a) 割引旅行	**b)** 旅行者、観光客	**c)** 多種、多様
d) 土産	**e)** 公共交通機関	**f)** 芸術作品

2 Reading Passage 🎧 7

Tourism is generally good. When people travel, they admire beautiful works of art, experience cultural differences, and taste new kinds of food. As the old saying goes, *variety is the spice of life.*

5 Tourism also has economic advantages. It helps the local economy. Tourists stay in hotels, eat in restaurants, and buy gifts and souvenirs in the stores.

Unfortunately tourism is not always good. Too much tourism – or *overtourism*, as it is sometimes called – is bad. It creates many problems,
10 especially for the local residents. The streets are crowded. Too many people use public transportation.

Some tourists are rude. They make too much noise, especially if they drink too much. They leave plastic bags and bottles on the streets. Often they do not respect local customs.

15 Overtourism is bad for the environment. Tourist buses increase air pollution, and cruise ships harm the ocean. Too many tourists can destroy beautiful beaches. Now many cities want to solve this problem. Here are some examples.

Venice plans to stop large cruise ships from sailing down the Grand Canal.
20 Dubrovnik, one of the film locations for *Game of Thrones*, wants to limit the number of visitors. In 2018, Thailand closed the beaches at Maya Bay because of overtourism.

Travel agencies also want to help. Now they have special discount tours for off-season travel. They advertise active vacations with hiking, sailing or
25 fishing. They support eco-tourism – tourism that is good for you and the environment.

Overtourism is a big problem. Do you want to help? Then please be a polite, eco-friendly tourist.

(Words: 257)

Notes

tourism: 観光旅行 **admire:** ～を賞賛する、～に感心してながめる **variety is the spice of life:** (諺)「変化は人生のスパイス」 **rude:** 礼儀を知らない **plastic bag(s):** ビニール［ナイロン］袋 **air pollution:** 大気汚染 **Venice:** ヴェニス (ベニス)(イタリア北東部	の都市) **The Grand Canal:** カナル・グランデ (大運河) **Dubrovnik:** ドゥブロヴニク (ドブロブニクまたはドブロヴニク) (南クロアチアの都市) ***Game of Thrones*:**『ゲーム・オブ・スローンズ』(小説及びドラマ) **Maya Bay:** マヤ湾 (タイのピピレイ島にある、映画『ザ・ビーチ』(2000) のロケ地)

3 Comprehension Questions

本文の内容に合っている文にはＴを、合っていない文にはＦを［　］に記入しましょう。

1. Tourism is good because it has only economic advantages. 　　　［　　］
2. Often tourists create many problems for the local residents. 　　　［　　］
3. Some cities have plans to control overtourism. 　　　［　　］
4. Overtourism must be controlled because it is a threat to the environment, the cultural treasures and the quality of life of local residents. 　　　［　　］

4 Guided Summary 🎵 8

次の英文は本文を要約したものです。(1) から (8) の空所に、下の (a) ～ (h) から適語を選んで記入し文を完成させましょう。

Today tourism is generally a (1)＿＿＿＿＿＿ factor. Tourists see works of art, (2)＿＿＿＿＿＿ cultural differences, and (3)＿＿＿＿＿＿ new kinds of food. Tourism is also a big (4)＿＿＿＿＿＿ industry. Overtourism is bad. It (5)＿＿＿＿＿＿ the environment, the cultural treasures and the (6)＿＿＿＿＿＿ of local residents. Some cities have plans to (7)＿＿＿＿＿＿ overtourism. Travel agencies now offer inexpensive (8)＿＿＿＿＿＿ tours as a way to stop overtourism.

📝 **Word List**

(a) threatens	**(b)** money-making	**(c)** off-season	**(d)** control
(e) taste	**(f)** positive	**(g)** quality of life	**(h)** experience

Overtourism is a Problem! | **9**

⑤ Essential Grammar 　現在形

▊ 現在形の形

英語では時制（現在・過去など）を動詞や助動詞の変化で表します。現在を示す場合は動詞を現在形にして使います。

1) be 動詞の現在形

人称 ＼ 数	単数	複数
1 人称	I am	We are
2 人称	You are	You are
3 人称	He She } is It	They are

　　ex 1) Tourism is generally good. (本文第 1 段落)
　　ex 2) Venice and Dubrovnik are sightseeing spots.

2) 一般動詞の現在形

① I, you, they などや複数の名詞が主語になる場合：動詞の原形 (現在形) を使う。
　　ex 3) They make too much noise. (本文第 4 段落)

② 3 人称単数が主語になる場合：動詞の語尾に -s または -es をつける。
　　ex 4) It helps the local economy. （ 本文第 2 段落 ）

> **-es をつける方法**
>
> (i) –s, -x, -sh, -ch で終わる動詞には es をつける。
> 　pass ⇒ passes,　mix ⇒ mixes,　wash ⇒ washes,
> 　watch ⇒ watches など
>
> (ii)「子音字 +y」で終わる動詞には、y を i に変えて -es をつける。
> 　cry ⇒ cries, try ⇒ tries など　* ただし「母音字 +y」で終わる動詞には、
> 　そのまま s をつける（play ⇒ plays, stay ⇒ stays など）。
>
> (iii)「子音字 +o」で終わる動詞には、-es をつける。
> 　do ⇒ does,　go ⇒ goes など

✎ Grammar Practice

次の日本語文に合うように英語文を完成させましょう。ただし文頭に来る語も小文字にしてあります。

　1. フロリダの気候は一般的に晴れです。

　　[weather / generally / the / Florida / sunny / in / is].

2. 私の趣味は、ハイキング、セーリングと魚釣りです。

   [fishing / sailing / my / hiking, / and / hobbies / are].

   _____

3. 私たちは文化的相違を体験します。[differences / experience / cultural / we].

   _____

4. ヴェニスには多くの観光客がいます。[has / tourists / lot / Venice / of / a].

   _____

6 Dialogue 🎧 9

音声を聞いて、日本語を参考にしながら空欄に聞き取った英語を書きましょう。

Junko is telling her American friend Billy about her trip to Italy.

Junko: _____. Great art, delicious food, and
（私のイタリア旅行はすごかったよ）

amazing fashion. _____.
（私はとても幸せだったの）

Billy: No bad experiences?

Junko: Well, Venice was a real challenge. In the summer, it's wall-to-wall
people on the streets and waterbuses, huge crowds at all the museums
and churches, and sky-high prices.

Billy: Next time, go in off-season. Then you can really enjoy Venice.

Junko: Yeah, that's good advice. Overtourism is a big problem in Venice.

Billy: So true! It's a threat to the environment, the art and the city.

_____.
（地元民は本当に怒っているよ）

Notes | **wall-to-wall:** 両側の壁まで一杯の　　**waterbus(es):** 水上バス

🌐 Did You Know?

ヴェニスには車はありません。この壮大な街は狭い橋でつながっている 118 の小さな島の上に造られています。この街を移動する最良の手段は、現地ではイタリア語で **vaporetto** と呼ぶ水上バスに乗ること、または徒歩です。もし贅沢をしたければ、水上タクシーに、あるいは、さらに素敵なゴンドラ（細長い平底船）に乗ってみましょう。それは、割高ですが、とてもロマンティックです。

⑦ Now It's Your Turn!

次の3つのトピックから1つ選び、回答例や Useful Expressions を参考にしながらパートナーと話し合ってみましょう。準備として、自分の意見をまとめておくと話し合いやすくなります。

1. Is overtourism a problem in important tourist spots in Japan?

2. Why is off-season tourism good for you?

3. What will you do if you can travel only during high season?

番号：☐

自分の意見 ....

....

....

回答例

1. I think (that) overtourism is a big problem in Japan because now there are so many foreign visitors. The tourist spots are too crowded, so it's no fun.

2. Off-season tourism is great because transportation, hotels and food cost less, so you save money. Also it's more fun because it's less crowded.

3. I don't want to deal with crowds, so I'll stay home, save money and wait until I can travel in off-season.

Useful Expressions

- Overtourism is a big problem in Japan because ...: オーバーツーリズムは日本で大きな問題です。なぜなら〜
- The tourist spots are too crowded, so ...: 観光地はとても混雑しています。ですから〜
- I prefer high season even if ...: たとえ〜でも、私は最も忙しい時期（ハイシーズン）のほうが好きです。
- I don't want to deal with crowds, so I'll ...: 大勢の人々とは関わり合いたくないので、私は〜

Chapter 3 — *Gender Equality in the Workplace*

世界で男女平等の流れがますます進んでいます。以前より女性の地位向上は進んでいますが、特に日本では、いまだあらゆる分野で男女が平等とは言いがたい状況です。

本章では職場での男女平等について考えます。男女平等のために私たちは何をすべきでしょうか？

1 Pre-Reading Questions 10

以下のイラストを参考にして、英文の下線部の意味を枠内の選択肢より選んで記号（a 〜 f）で答えましょう。

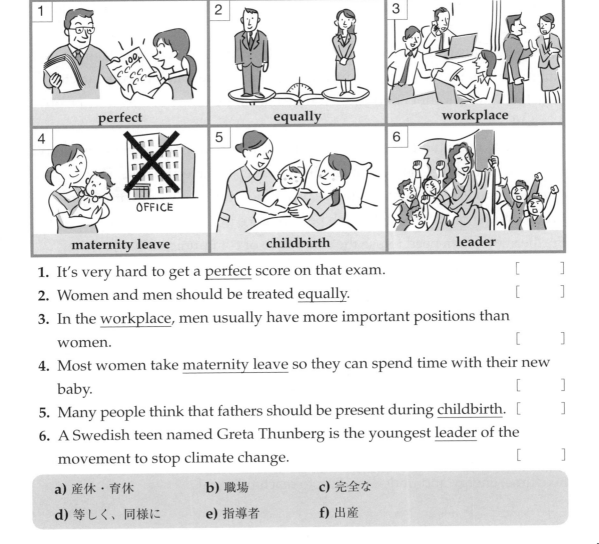

1. It's very hard to get a <u>perfect</u> score on that exam. [   ]
2. Women and men should be treated <u>equally</u>. [   ]
3. In the <u>workplace</u>, men usually have more important positions than women. [   ]
4. Most women take <u>maternity leave</u> so they can spend time with their new baby. [   ]
5. Many people think that fathers should be present during <u>childbirth</u>. [   ]
6. A Swedish teen named Greta Thunberg is the youngest <u>leader</u> of the movement to stop climate change. [   ]

a) 産休・育休	**b)** 職場	**c)** 完全な
d) 等しく、同様に	**e)** 指導者	**f)** 出産

Today people talk a lot about *gender equality*. In a perfect world, women and men would be treated equally. Unfortunately that's not true, even in highly developed countries!

5   Let's focus on the workplace where women often do not get equal treatment. They earn less than men, even when they do the same job. They are promoted less often than men. That's why there are still fewer women in top positions.

    There is also the problem of maternity leave and job security. Many 10 American women are not paid during maternity leave. Their job is protected only for 12 weeks after childbirth. If they take more time off, they may be out of a job!

    Clearly this situation is unfair. What can we do to achieve gender equality?

    First of all, men should change the way they behave at work. They 15 must learn to listen to what women say and be willing to work with them. Promotions should be based on job performance rather than gender. Furthermore, men need to use the same style of communication when they speak to both female and male staff.

    Second, women have to change their behavior in the workplace. They 20 must not be afraid to express their opinions. They should remember that it's OK to disagree. If women want to be leaders, they have to act like leaders – strong, positive and polite.

    Third, companies should have plans that promote gender equality such as paid maternity leave, flexible working schedules and working from home. 25 Gender awareness programs are also helpful.

    Gender equality in the workplace is not an impossible dream, but it will take time, energy and understanding to reach this goal.

(Words: 275)

equal treatment: 平等な待遇
promote: 昇進させる
job security: 雇用保障、仕事の保障

gender awareness programs: 性別に関する啓発活動

③ Comprehension Questions

本文の内容に合っている文には T を、合っていない文には F を ［　］に記入しましょう。

1. In the workplace, it's more difficult for a woman to reach top positions.
   ［　］

2. To promote gender equality, both women and men have to change how they behave at work. ［　］

3. Companies need to have programs to promote gender equality. ［　］

4. Gender equality is an impossible dream because it will take too much time, energy and understanding. ［　］

④ Guided Summary 🎵 12

次の英文は本文を要約したものです。(1) から (8) の空所に、下の (a) ～ (h) から適語を選んで記入し文を完成させましょう。

Today even in (1)＿＿＿＿＿＿ countries, women and men are not treated equally. Women earn less, and get promoted less often. Many companies do not give women paid (2)＿＿＿＿＿. To achieve gender equality, (3)＿＿＿＿＿ should be based on (4)＿＿＿＿＿ rather than (5)＿＿＿＿＿. Both women and men need to change how they (6)＿＿＿＿＿ at work. Companies need to develop plans that promote gender (7)＿＿＿＿＿. It will take time, energy and (8)＿＿＿＿＿ to reach this goal.

📓 Word List

(a) behave	**(b)** promotions	**(c)** developed	**(d)** understanding
(e) equality	**(f)** gender	**(g)** maternity leave	**(h)** job performance

⑤ Essential Grammar 　助動詞

助動詞は、動詞の原形の前に置き、その動詞にいろいろな意味をつけ加える働きをします。

can

can は「〜できる」(可能)、「ありうる」(可能性) などの意味を表します。

ex 1) What can we do to achieve gender equality? (本文第 4 段落)

should

should は、何をしたらよいかについて助言する時に使い、「〜すべきである」という意味を表します。

ex 2) Men should change the way they behave at work. (本文第 5 段落)

must

must は、する必要があることを表す時に使い、「〜しなくてはならない」という意味を表します。

ex 3) They must learn to listen to what women say. (本文第 5 段落)

　　must の否定形 must not (mustn't) は「〜してはならない」という意味を表します。

ex 4) They must not be afraid to express their opinions. (本文第 6 段落)

　　have to も must と同様「〜しなくてはならない」の意味を表します。

ex 5) Women have to change their behavior in the workplace. (本文第 6 段落)

may

「〜かもしれない」(推量)、「〜してもよい」(許可) が may の代表的な意味です。

ex 6) They may be out of a job. (本文第 3 段落)

🖊 Grammar Practice

次の日本語文に合うように英語文を完成させましょう。ただし文頭に来る語も小文字にしてあります。

1. その文書をお送りいただけると助かります。

   [the document / if / you / would be / helpful / send me / it / could].

   _____

2. 間違っているかもしれませんが、私は彼を信じたい。

   [but I / wrong, / trust / be / want to / him / may / I].

   _____

3. 彼は父親の意見を聞くことを学ばなければなりません。

[his father's / must / to / he / opinion / to / learn / listen].

_____

4. 初心者ドライバーということをあなたは忘れてはいけません。

[should / that / remember / you / beginner driver / are / you / a].

_____

6 Dialogue 🔊 13

音声を聞いて、日本語を参考にしながら空欄に聞き取った英語を書きましょう。

Kazue is talking to her American fiancé Bobby about her job interview. She is very upset.

Bobby: Kazue, honey! What happened? Please stop crying!

Kazue: Oh, Bobby, I didn't get the job. I'm really upset. The interview was going so well – they loved my CV – and then (sob, sob, sob) …

Bobby: Then what? Come on, and _____.
（何があったか教えて）

Kazue: Well, they asked me if _____, I was planning to have
（将来いつか）

kids!

Bobby: What? They'd never ask a guy that question!

Kazue: You're right. It's so unfair. Women and men _____

_____.
（同じように扱われるべき）

Bobby: Don't worry! Next time you're going to interview with a company that has a gender awareness program.

Notes | **CV:** = curriculum vitae（履歴書）　　**sob:** すすり泣く

🌐 Did You Know?

多くの企業が「性別に関する啓発活動」に取り組み、昔からあるステレオタイプや偏見の問題を解決しようとしています。例えば、「女性は理系の分野は得意ではない」や「女性は感情的なので管理職に向かない」や「女性は子どもを持つと働くのをやめる」といったものです。これらの偏見を取り除くために、より多くの人が問題意識を持ち、男女平等のための活動に参加することが重要です。

⑦ Now It's Your Turn!

次の 3 つのトピックから 1 つ選び、回答例や Useful Expressions を参考にしながらパートナーと話し合ってみましょう。準備として、自分の意見をまとめておくと話し合いやすくなります。

1. Do you think that women should get paid maternity leave?

2. Do you think that women and men should change the way they behave at work?

3. Do you think that gender equality is an impossible dream?

番号： ☐

自分の意見 ....

....

....

回答例

1. Definitely! It's not fair to make a woman choose between career and family. After all, children are our future!

2. Yes! Men have to learn to listen to women, and women have to learn to express their opinions. Then things will get better.

3. No, I don't. It's not going to be easy, but with time and understanding, it will happen.

Useful Expressions

- It's not fair to ...: ～することは公平ではありません。
- Men have to learn to listen to women.: 男性は女性の意見を聞くことを学ばなければなりません。
- Things will get better.: 物事はよくなっていきます。
- It's not going to be easy, but ...: それは簡単ではないでしょう。しかし～

Chapter 4

Changing Definitions of Beauty

　あなたは、何に対して「美しい」と思いますか？　また、「美しい」と定義するのに基準があると思いますか？　時代や地域、また人の価値観によって、「美」に対する考え方は異なります。

　本章では、移り変わる「美の定義」について考えてみましょう。

1 Pre-Reading Questions 🔘 14

以下のイラストを参考にして、英文の下線部の意味を枠内の選択肢より選んで記号（a 〜 f）で答えましょう。

| 1 dictionary | 2 beauty | 3 thin |
| 4 age | 5 makeup | 6 hire |

1. A <u>dictionary</u> explains the meaning of words, including ones with new meanings. 　　　　　　　　　[　]
2. The definition of <u>beauty</u> changes from country to country. 　[　]
3. Most fashion models are very <u>thin</u>. 　[　]
4. Today some models are over the <u>age</u> of 50. 　[　]
5. Now women with darker skin can easily find <u>makeup</u>. 　[　]
6. The company has to <u>hire</u> more young people. 　[　]

| **a)** 辞書 | **b)** 痩せた | **c)** 美 |
| **d)** 化粧 | **e)** 年齢 | **f)** 雇う |

The dictionary defines *beauty* as something or someone, usually a woman, that is lovely to look at. But what people consider *beautiful* changes from generation to generation and from country to country. As an old proverb reminds us, *beauty*
5 *is in the eye of the beholder.*

Now let's look at the definition of female beauty in the West. For many years, a beautiful woman was supposed to be thin, fit, young and white. The Internet, TV, movies and magazines have shown pictures of these "perfect" women. The message was clear. If you want to be beautiful, you had to look
10 like them.

This single standard of beauty is unrealistic because most women don't look like the models. Furthermore, now that Western societies are becoming more ethnically diverse, the definition has to include women with different body types, different skin colors, different hairstyles and different ages. In
15 other words, *good-bye* to the single standard and *hello* to diversity.

The fashion industry is also supporting diversity in beauty. Women with full figures can find fashionable clothes, often by top designers. Women with darker skin have a wide choice of makeup and skincare products. Women over 50 as well as women with disabilities are being hired as models.
20 Unlike countries in the West, Japan does not have a diverse population. In recent years, however, Japanese society is being "globalized" because there are more tourists from abroad, more foreign workers and more international events such as the Olympics.

Do you think that the traditional Japanese definition of beauty needs to be
25 changed? Should it be more diverse?

(Words: 263)

proverb: ことわざ、格言
beholder: 見る人（Beauty is in the eye of the beholder. 「美は見る人の目の中にある」から「蓼食う虫も好きずき」の意のことわざ）

unrealistic: 非現実的な、現実離れした
ethnically: 民族的には
women with full figures: 大きいサイズの（服を着る）女性

③ Comprehension Questions

本文の内容に合っている文には T を、合っていない文には F を ［　　］に記入しましょう。

1. What people consider beautiful changes from generation to generation and from country to country. ［　　］
2. Throughout history, the definition of beauty has never changed. ［　　］
3. Today in Western countries, it's difficult for women with full figures to find fashionable clothes. ［　　］
4. Today Japanese society is less diverse than in the past. ［　　］

④ Guided Summary 🎧 16

次の英文は本文を要約したものです。(1) から (8) の空所に、下の (a) 〜 (h) から適語を選んで記入し文を完成させましょう。

The definition of what people consider beautiful changes from (1)_____ to generation and from country to country. Until (2)_____, a beautiful woman in the West was supposed to be thin, (3)_____, young and white. Now Western societies are more (4)_____ diverse, so the definition of beauty has changed. It now includes women with different body types, different skin colors, different (5)_____ and different ages. The (6)_____ industry is supporting (7)_____ in beauty. Will the Japanese definition of beauty change because of (8)_____?

📝 Word List

(a) fit   (b) ethnically   (c) fashion   (d) globalization
(e) generation (f) diversity   (g) recently   (h) hairstyles

⑤ Essential Grammar 　進行形

一時的な動作の継続を表すために使うのが進行形です。進行形は、「be 動詞＋動詞の現在分詞 (-ing)」の形で表します。

▌現在進行形

ある一時的な動作が、現在行われつつある時（現在行われている時）に使われます。「am/are/is ＋動詞の現在分詞 (-ing)」です。

ex 1) Western societies <u>are becoming</u> more ethnically diverse. (本文第 3 段落)
ex 2) The fashion industry <u>is supporting</u> diversity in beauty. (本文 4 段落)

▌過去進行形

ある一時的な動作が、過去のある時点で行われつつあったことを表します。「was/were ＋動詞の現在分詞 (-ing)」です。

ex 3) When I visited him in his room, he <u>was doing</u> his homework. (私が彼の部屋に彼を訪問した際、彼は宿題をしているところでした)

▌現在完了進行形

過去のある時から現在までの動作の継続を強調するために用いられます。have been -ing で「ずっと～している」というニュアンスを表します。

ex 4) English <u>has</u> always <u>been changing</u>. (英語はずっと変わってきています)

▌受動態の進行形 (進行形の受動態)

「～されつつある」と受け身の状態が進行をしていることを表す形で、「am/are/is/was/were being ＋過去分詞」の形をとります。

ex 5) They <u>are being hired</u> as models. (本文第 4 段落)
ex 6) Japanese society <u>is being globalized</u>. (本文第 5 段落)

✎ Grammar Practice

次の日本語文に合うように英語文を完成させましょう。ただし文頭に来る語も小文字にしてあります。

1. 状況がますます悪化していると私は思います。

   [is / worse / the situation / I think / becoming / that / worse / and].

   _____

2. 食品業界は有機栽培の農家を支援し続けています。

   [has / farmers / food / supporting / organic / been / industry / the].

   _____

3. 彼の会社は不況により打撃を受けています。

[company / recession / being / his / hurt / the / is / by].

_____

4. 私が彼を訪問したとき、彼は彼女とおしゃべりをしていました。

[his girlfriend / when / was / visited him, / I / with / he / chatting].

_____

❻ Dialogue 🎧 17

音声を聞いて、日本語を参考にしながら空欄に聞き取った英語を書きましょう。

Akiko is a Japanese exchange student in the US. She is having coffee with her American friend Eddie.

Eddie: So _____, Akiko?
          (今日はどうでしたか)

Akiko: Really fun! I went to the mall with my friend Sandy. She was looking
          for a dress _____.
                      (彼女の友だちの結婚式に着ていく)

Eddie: I hope she found one she likes.

Akiko: Yes, she did, but _____. The ones she tried on first
                            (かなり時間がかかった)

          were too small, so we went to the Plus Size department.

Eddie: The WHAT department? I've never heard of that.

Akiko: Well, it's for girls with full figures – like Sandy. There were so many
          cool dresses there. She got something really special.

Eddie: Glad the two of you had fun.

7 Now It's Your Turn!

次の3つのトピックから1つ選び、回答例や Useful Expressions を参考にしながらパートナーと話し合ってみましょう。準備として、自分の意見をまとめておくと話し合いやすくなります。

1. Do you think that a single standard of beauty is good or bad?
2. Why is the fashion industry supporting diversity in beauty?
3. Do you think that the Japanese definition of beauty needs to be changed?

番号：

自分の意見

....

....

....

回答例

1. In my opinion, a single standard is bad. It's unrealistic and also unfair because most women don't look like the models in pictures.

2. The fashion industry is supporting diversity in beauty so that all women can find clothes and makeup to make them feel beautiful. I think it's great.

3. No, I don't. Almost everybody in Japan – that is, 98.5% of the population – is Japanese, so there's no need to change the definition.

Useful Expressions

- In my opinion, a single standard is ...: 私の意見としては、単一の規準は〜
- There's no need to change the definition.: 定義を変える必要はありません。
- The definition has to be changed.: 定義は変えられなければなりません。
- As Japanese society becomes more ethnically diverse ...: 日本の社会が民族的により多様化されるにつれて、〜

Chapter 5
Romeo and Juliet: A Tragic Story about Intolerance

ウィリアム・シェイクスピア（William Shakespeare, 1564-1616）の不朽の名作『ロミオとジュリエット』（*Romeo and Juliet*, 1595年頃）については、聞いたことがあるでしょうか。演劇や映画で見たことがある人もいるでしょう。この恋愛悲劇は、星の巡りの悪い（star-crossed）恋人たちの世界で最も有名なラブストーリーの1つです。

1 Pre-Reading Questions 18

以下のイラストを参考にして、英文の下線部の意味を枠内の選択肢より選んで記号（a 〜 f）で答えましょう。

1 fall in love	2 peace	3 bury someone
4 religions	5 disagree	6 refuse to discuss

1. Romeo and Juliet <u>fell in love</u>, and wanted to marry.   [   ]
2. The dove is a symbol of <u>peace</u>.   [   ]
3. The parents <u>buried</u> Romeo and Juliet side by side.   [   ]
4. There are many different <u>religions</u> in the world.   [   ]
5. People often <u>disagree</u> when they discuss politics.   [   ]
6. After the argument, they <u>refused to discuss</u> anything.   [   ]

a) 話し合うことを拒む	**b)** 反対する	**c)** 人を埋葬する
d) 平和	**e)** 恋に落ちる、ぞっこん惚れる	**f)** 宗教

In the 13th century, the northern Italian city of Verona was dangerous. Two powerful families – the Capulets and the Montagues – were political enemies. That's why there was so much violence and intolerance in the city.

5   One day Romeo Montague met a beautiful girl named Juliet Capulet. The two young people immediately fell in love. This love was dangerous because the parents of Romeo and Juliet hated each other.

    There was only one way for Romeo and Juliet to solve this problem. They had to marry secretly and leave Verona forever. Unfortunately their plan did 10 not work out. So death was the only way for them to be together.

    When the Capulets and the Montagues learned the terrible news, they understood their mistake. Their intolerance was the reason for their children's death. Now it was time for the two families to stop fighting and start talking. As a sign of peace, they buried Romeo and Juliet side by side.

15   Intolerance is dangerous. It destroys people, families and societies. Sometimes, as in the case of Romeo and Juliet, the reason is politics. Other times, it's religion, race or gender.

    What can you do to stop intolerance? First of all, don't be afraid to talk about the problem. Second, listen carefully, and try to understand the other 20 person's ideas. If you don't communicate, you can't find a solution.

    It's OK if people disagree. It's not OK if they refuse to discuss their differences. Communication can change intolerance into tolerance. This is the lesson we learn from the story of Romeo and Juliet.

(Words: 259)

Notes | **Verona:** ヴェローナ (ベローナ)(イタリア北部の都市)   ピュレット家とモンタギュー家
intolerance: 不寛容、不耐性
the Capulets and the Montagues: キャ

③ Comprehension Questions

本文の内容に合っている文には T を、合っていない文には F を [   ] に記入しましょう。

1. Romeo and Juliet immediately fell in love because their families were political rivals.   [   ]

2. The parents were angry because Romeo and Juliet did not get married.
                                                                          [   ]

3. Intolerance is caused only by political differences.   [   ]

4. The only way to stop intolerance is to reach out and talk about your differences.   [   ]

④ Guided Summary   🎧 20

次の英文は本文を要約したものです。(1) から (8) の空所に、下の (a) 〜 (h) から適語を選んで記入し文を完成させましょう。

The love story of Romeo and Juliet shows that (1)_____ is very
(2)_____. The two young people immediately fell in love. They
planned to marry secretly because their parents were political (3)_____.
Due to a series of unfortunate (4)_____, their plan to marry secretly
failed. So death was the only way to be together. Intolerance can
(5)_____ individuals, families and societies. The cause can be politics,
(6)_____, race or gender. To (7)_____ intolerance into tolerance,
we need to (8)_____ so that we can find a solution.

🗐 Word List

(a) destroy   (b) change   (c) intolerance   (d) problems
(e) dangerous (f) communicate (g) religion   (h) enemies

⑤ Essential Grammar   過去形

英語では時制（現在・過去など）を動詞や助動詞の変化で表します。過去を示す場合は動詞を過去形にして使います。

過去形の形

1) be 動詞の過去形

人称 ＼ 数	単数	複数
1 人称	I was	We were
2 人称	You were	You were
3 人称	He She } was It	They were

ex 1）The northern Italian city of Verona was dangerous. (本文第 1 段落)
ex 2）Two powerful families were political enemies. (本文第 1 段落)

2) 一般動詞の過去形

過去形にする方法

(i) 原形に -ed をつけて過去形にする。
ex 3）The Capulets and the Montagues learned the terrible news. (本文第 4 段落)

(ii) 原形が e で終わる動詞には -d をつける。
ex 4）The parents of Romeo and Juliet hated each other. (本文第 2 段落)

(iii) 語尾が「子音字 +y」で終わる動詞の場合は、語尾の y を i に変えて、-ed をつける。
　＊ただし「母音字 +y」で終わる動詞には、そのまま ed をつける。

(iv)「1 つの短母音字 +1 つの子音字」で終わる単音節の動詞の場合には、語尾の子音字を重ねて -ed をつける。ex 5）They planned to marry secretly.

(v) 不規則変化をする。
ex 6）Romeo Montague met a beautiful girl named Juliet Capulet.(本文第 2 段落)
　　　不規則変化をする動詞は頻出動詞が多い。

✏ Grammar Practice

次の日本語文に合うように英語文を完成させましょう。ただし文頭に来る語も小文字にしてあります。

1. その問題の根源は、お金でした。[the / the / of / was / root / money / problem].

2. 彼らはお互いに話すのを拒みました。
[refused / speak / other / they / each / with / to].

3. あの日、何か不思議なことが起きました。

[mysterious / something / happened / day / that].

_____

4. 信仰がこの問題の原因でした。

[the / problem / cause / was / this / religion / of].

_____

 **Dialogue** 21

音声を聞いて、日本語を参考にしながら空欄に聞き取った英語を書きましょう。

Nicole is talking about intolerance with Takashi, a Japanese exchange student at the University of Florida.

Takashi: In my English class, we just finished reading Shakespeare's _Romeo and Juliet_. Those kids really had a tough time. I mean, having to deal with families who hated each other.

Nicole: Their love story is so-o-o tragic. The parents really messed up their kids' lives. The two families should have worked out their differences and _____ Romeo and Juliet _____.
(結婚させてあげる)

Takashi: When people are intolerant, bad things happen. Intolerance destroys individuals, families and even societies.

Nicole: Yeah! Just look around at _____ today.
(世界で起きていること)
People are fighting and killing each other. Just insane!

Takashi: And how about the refugee crisis? Such a human tragedy!

Nicole: I agree completely. People gotta talk to each other and find a solution. That's _____.
(平和に暮らす唯一の方法)

Notes | **tragic:** 悲劇的　　**insane:** ばかげている　　**refugee crisis:** 難民危機
gotta: ～しなきゃならない (got to のくだけた形)

 Did You Know?

インドのアグラにあるタージマハルは、世界で最も美しい建造物の１つです。統治者シャー・ジャハーンは、彼の愛する妻ムムターズ・マハルを偲んで豪華な墓をつくるよう彼の技師たちに命じました。また、ローマの将軍マーク・アンソニーはエジプトの魅力的な女王クレオパトラに首ったけになりました。ローマ人たちは怒り、エジプトを滅ぼそうと決めました。クレオパトラ軍が敗退した時、愛する２人は永遠に一緒にいられるように自殺をしました。

7 Now It's Your Turn!

次の３つのトピックから１つ選び、回答例や Useful Expressions を参考にしながらパートナーと話し合ってみましょう。準備として、自分の意見をまとめておくと話し合いやすくなります。

1. What did you learn from the tragic story of Romeo and Juliet?
2. Do you think that it's OK to disagree?
3. Give some examples of intolerance caused by forces such as religion or politics.

番号： ☐

自分の意見 ....
....
....

回答例

1. Well, I learned that communication is really important. Romeo and Juliet wouldn't have died if their parents had discussed their differences.

2. Of course! People have different opinions. That's natural. Just listen, be polite, and don't get into an argument!

3. Well, let's take the case of India where there is often religious intolerance between the Hindus and the Muslims.

Useful Expressions

- Romeo and Juliet wouldn't have died if ...: もし〜だったなら、ロミオとジュリエットは死ななかったでしょう。
- People have different opinions.: 人は異なる意見を持っています。
- Well, let's take the case of ...: そうですね、〜の件を考えてみましょう。
- There is a lot of intolerance between A and B.: AとBの間には多くの不寛容があります。

Chapter 6

Nature and Health

あなたは登山やハイキングなど自然に触れることが好きですか？ 近年、欧米において森林浴が注目を集めています。自然により触れることで、ストレス発散につながり、心や体によい影響をあたえることが分かってきています。

本章では、自然と健康の関係を考えてみましょう。

1 Pre-Reading Questions 22

以下のイラストを参考にして、英文の下線部の意味を枠内の選択肢より選んで記号（a ～ f）で答えましょう。

| 1 patient | 2 medical chart | 3 prescription |
| 4 medicine | 5 outdoors | 6 relax |

1. A <u>patient</u> is a sick person who needs medical care.　　[　　]
2. The doctor looked at Yoshi's <u>medical chart</u>.　　[　　]
3. The doctor wrote a <u>prescription</u> for his sick patient.　　[　　]
4. Always follow the directions when you take <u>medicine</u>.　　[　　]
5. Spending time <u>outdoors</u> is good for your health.　　[　　]
6. I <u>relax</u> when I listen to music.　　[　　]

a) くつろぐ	b) 屋外（で）	c) 薬
d) カルテ	e) 患者	f) 処方箋

Nature and Health | 31

The doctor listened carefully as the patient described her problems. She was stressed and tired because she was not sleeping well. After reviewing her medical chart, the doctor wrote a prescription, but it wasn't for
5 medicine. Instead it was a prescription for his patient to spend time outdoors.

Today more and more doctors in the US and Europe are writing these so-called *nature prescriptions*. Spending time outdoors, especially in a green area like a park, is good for both the body and the mind. It lowers blood pressure, reduces stress, and increases energy. Some mental health professionals do
10 outdoor therapy sessions because patients relax when they are close to nature.

Doctors insist that children who spend time outdoors are healthier than those who don't. Playing outdoors makes them physically stronger. It rests their brain from the stress of school. When they are playing, they can't use their smartphones.

15 Are these nature prescriptions really necessary? Why don't doctors just tell the patient to take a walk in the park? The answer may surprise you. Patients are more motivated to follow the doctor's "orders" when they have a prescription.

Robert Zarr, a doctor in Washington D.C., believes that nature
20 prescriptions should be part of healthcare. He recently founded a non-profit organization called *ParksRx America*. His goal is to encourage people of all ages to spend time outdoors – in their local parks as well as the national ones.

You don't need a nature prescription to enjoy the outdoors. You can go forest bathing or do outdoor yoga. Just remember that connecting with nature
25 is good for both the body and the mind.

(Words: 269)

Notes

blood pressure: 血圧
therapy session: セラピーセッション、治療セッション
motivate: やる気にさせる、意欲を起こさせる
Robert Zarr: ロバート・ザール（小児科医。

ParksRx America の創始者）
non-profit: 非営利の
ParksRx America: Robert Zarr が興した非営利団体。Rx は prescription の意味。
forest bathing: 森林浴

3 Comprehension Questions

本文の内容に合っている文には T を、合っていない文には F を ［　　］ に記入しましょう。

1. Spending time outdoors is good for your health because it reduces your stress, and increases your energy. ［　　］

2. It's good for children to play outdoors with their smartphones. ［　　］

3. Spending time outdoors is important only for children. ［　　］

4. If you don't have a nature prescription, you can't enjoy the outdoors.

［　　］

4 Guided Summary 🎧 24

次の英文は本文を要約したものです。(1) から (8) の空所に、下の (a) ～ (h) から適語を選んで記入し文を完成させましょう。

Today many doctors in the US and Europe write nature (1)_____ for their (2)_____. Spending time outdoors, especially in a green (3)_____ like a park, is good for your body and your (4)_____. Children who spend time (5)_____ are (6)_____ than those who don't. But remember that you don't need a nature prescription to (7)_____ nature. Just go outdoors and (8)_____ with nature.

Word List

(a) mind   (b) healthier   (c) patients   (d) enjoy
(e) prescriptions   (f) connect   (g) area   (h) outdoors

⑤ Essential Grammar   動名詞

動名詞は、動詞と名詞の働きを兼ねそなえたもので、動詞を -ing 形にして「〜すること」という意味を表します。

▌動名詞の働き

①主語：<u>Walking</u> is good for your health. (歩くことはあなたの健康にとってよいことです)

② be 動詞の補語：My hobby is <u>listening</u> to music. (私の趣味は音楽を聴くことです)

③他動詞の目的語：We enjoyed <u>talking</u> with her. (私たちは彼女と話すことを楽しみました)

④前置詞の目的語：She is interested in <u>taking</u> pictures. (彼女は写真を撮ることに興味があります)

ex 1) After <u>reviewing</u> her medical chart, the doctor wrote a prescription. (本文第 1 段落)

reviewing (her medical chart) が前置詞 after の後に置かれ、「〜を見た後」と after の目的語となっています。(⇒④前置詞の目的語)

ex 2) <u>Spending</u> time outdoors is good for both the body and the mind. (本文第 2 段落)

spending time outdoors「屋外で時を過ごすことは」と主語になっています。(⇒①主語)

ex 3) <u>Connecting</u> with nature is good for both the body and the mind. (本文第 6 段落)

connecting with nature「自然とつながることは」と主語になっています。(⇒①主語)

▌動名詞を使う頻出表現

go -ing (〜しに行く)

ex 4) You can <u>go</u> forest <u>bathing</u>. (本文第 6 段落)

他に、go shopping, go fishing, go snowboarding, go skiing, go skating, go hiking, go hunting, go swimming などもよく使われます。

✎ Grammar Practice

次の日本語文に合うように英語文を完成させましょう。ただし文頭に来る語も小文字にしてあります。

1. 売上高を検討した後、上司は私の昇給を決めた。

[my boss / after / to / my salary / the sales figures, / reviewing / decided / raise].

_____

2. 私はあなたがいつ野球をやめたのか知りたいです。

[want / when / playing baseball / know / to / you / stopped / I].

_____

3. 数学を勉強することは、あなたの将来に有益です。

[math / your / helpful / learning / for / is / future].

_____

4. 私の趣味の1つは、大画面で映画を見ることです。

[a big screen / watching / one / on / my hobbies / is / movies / of].

_____

6 Dialogue 25

音声を聞いて、日本語を参考にしながら空欄に聞き取った英語を書きましょう。

Kiyoshi, a Japanese exchange student in the US, is talking to his friend Debbie about her doctor's appointment.

Kiyoshi: So what did the doctor say?

Debbie: Well, she told me that my BP was a bit high, but probably because I'm very stressed. So she gave me a nature prescription.

Kiyoshi: What? _____ a nature prescription.
（今まで〜を聞いたことがない）

Debbie: Well, now you have. I have to spend 30 minutes outdoors three times a week. _____ my stress and lower
（それが〜を減らす手助けをしてくれる）
my BP.

Kiyoshi: Come on, Debbie. You don't need a nature prescription for that. Just take a walk in the park!

Debbie: Easier said than done! With a prescription, _____
（私はもっと〜をやる気になる）
_____ follow the doctor's orders.

Kiyoshi: Well, if you say so. I just want you to feel better!

Note | BP: = blood pressure

Did You Know?

昔に比べ、今の子どもたちは屋外で遊ばなくなったといいます。理由は何でしょうか？　まず、多くの家族が都市部に住むようになり、子どもが遊ぶ屋外の場所が少なくなったことが挙げられます。第2に、多くの子どもが、SNS、ネットサーフィン、テレビゲームに時間を多く費やすようになりました。また、放課後の習い事や塾に行くことが多くなり、子どもたちに遊ぶ時間がなくなってきていることも原因のようです。

7 Now It's Your Turn!

次の３つのトピックから１つ選び、回答例や Useful Expressions を参考にしながらパートナーと話し合ってみましょう。準備として、自分の意見をまとめておくと話し合いやすくなります。

1. Do you think that nature prescriptions are a good idea?
2. Why is it important for children to play outdoors?
3. Why is forest bathing good for your health?

番号： ☐

自分の意見

....

....

....

回答例

1. No. You don't need a nature prescription to go outdoors. All you have to do is take a walk in the park.

2. Playing outdoors makes kids stronger and healthier. It's good for their body, just as school is good for their mind.

3. Forest bathing lets you connect with nature so you can forget the stress of daily life. It relaxes and calms you.

Useful Expressions

- With a prescription, people are more motivated to ...: 処方箋があれば人はより意欲的に〜をします。
- All you have to do is ...: あなたがしなければならないのは〜だけです。
- Playing outdoors makes kids stronger and healthier.: 屋外で遊ぶことは子どもをより強く健康にします。
- Forest bathing lets you connect with nature.: 森林浴によってあなたは自然とのつながりを持てます。
- Forest bathing is really great for people who ...: 森林浴は〜な人にとって、本当にすばらしいです。

Chapter 7

Golden Years and Silver Divorces

定年退職後の老後のことを、英語ではgolden years と言います。仕事から解放され、娯楽で溢れるいわゆる「黄金時代」ですが、実際にはすべての人にとってgoldenとはいかないようです。

本章では、定年退職後の老後におこる「熟年離婚」について考えてみましょう。

① Pre-Reading Questions 26

以下のイラストを参考にして、英文の下線部の意味を枠内の選択肢より選んで記号（a ～ f）で答えましょう。

| 1 divorce | 2 marriage | 3 gambling |
| 4 drinking | 5 pay the bills | 6 depression |

1. The mother took their daughter after the <u>divorce</u>.　[　　]
2. This is Maria's second <u>marriage</u>.　She divorced her first husband.　[　　]
3. If you like <u>gambling</u>, then go to Las Vegas!　[　　]
4. After work, many businessmen go <u>drinking</u> with their friends.　[　　]
5. If you lose your job, it's hard to <u>pay the bills</u>.　[　　]
6. Loneliness often causes <u>depression</u>.　[　　]

| a) 鬱（うつ） | b) 賭（か）け事、賭博（とばく） | c) 結婚 |
| d) 生活費を払う | e) 飲酒 | f) 離婚 |

2 Reading Passage 27

Many people dream about the *golden years* when they are supposed to enjoy their retirement. Unfortunately dreams don't always come true. Sometimes the golden years are full of health problems, financial worries and family troubles.

5   There is another reason why the golden years aren't always *golden*. In the last 20 years, the divorce rate among people over 50 has increased in the US, Europe and Japan. These are the so-called *silver divorces* because older women and men often have *silver* (gray) hair.

Why do couples divorce after many years of marriage? Maybe they have
10 fallen "out" of love, and want to find a new partner. Perhaps they have grown apart, and no longer share the same interests. There may be serious problems such as gambling, drinking or arguing.

Silver divorces don't work out if people can't adjust to change. They complain that living alone is expensive. They have to cut costs so they can pay
15 the bills. Household chores can be a challenge, especially for men.

Silver divorces can cause emotional problems. People feel lonely if they have no friends and bored if they have no interests. Loneliness and boredom often lead to depression.

Silver divorces work out well when people are not afraid of change. With
20 a positive attitude, they are ready to start their "new" life.

Some decide to remarry. Others stay single so they can follow their dreams. They go back to school, make new friends, travel to foreign countries, do volunteer work, or even start second careers. These silver divorcees enjoy their golden years.

25   What's your opinion about silver divorces?

(Words: 264)

financial worries: お金の心配、金銭上の
悩み
grow apart: 距離ができる、心が離れる
household chores: 家事

boredom: 退屈
work out: なんとかなる、うまくいく
remarry: 再婚する
divorcee: 離婚者

③ Comprehension Questions

本文の内容に合っている文には T を、合っていない文には F を [　] に記入しましょう。

1. In the past 20 years, there has been an increase in the number of the
    so-called silver divorces. [　　]

2. Couples always divorce when there are serious problems such as
    gambling, drinking or arguing. [　　]

3. It's not a good idea to get a silver divorce if you don't have enough
    money to live alone. [　　]

4. People who get a silver divorce always enjoy their golden years. [　　]

④ Guided Summary 28

次の英文は本文を要約したものです。(1) から (8) の空所に、下の (a) 〜 (h) から適語を選んで
記入し文を完成させましょう。

In the last 20 years, the divorce (1)＿＿＿＿＿＿＿ among people over 50 has
(2)＿＿＿＿＿＿＿. These are the so-called silver divorces. Couples divorce after
many years of (3)＿＿＿＿＿＿ for a variety of reasons such as falling in love
with another person, gambling, drinking or (4)＿＿＿＿＿＿. Silver divorces
don't work out well when people don't (5)＿＿＿＿＿＿ to change. Sometimes
they become (6)＿＿＿＿＿＿. Some silver divorces, however, work out well
because the divorcees build new, (7)＿＿＿＿＿＿ lives for themselves. Then
they really (8)＿＿＿＿＿＿ their golden years.

🗒 Word List

(a) adjust	**(b)** arguing	**(c)** enjoy	**(d)** exciting
(e) marriage	**(f)** rate	**(g)** depressed	**(h)** increased

⑤ Essential Grammar 　否定文

「〜である」「〜する」という肯定形に対し、「〜ではない」「〜しない」という否定形があり、not などの否定語を用いて、主語と述語の結びつきを否定するのが否定文です。

I like English. (私は英語が好きです) ［肯定文］
I do <u>not</u> [<u>don't</u>] like English. (私は英語が好きではありません) ［否定文］

主な否定語には次のようなものがあります。

not

最も一般的に用いられる否定語

    ex 1) Silver divorces <u>don't</u> [=do <u>not</u>] work out. (本文第 4 段落)
    ex 2) People <u>can't</u> [=can <u>not</u>, <u>cannot</u>] adjust to change. (本文第 4 段落)

no

not よりもやや強い否定語

    ex 3) They have <u>no</u> friends. (本文第 5 段落)

not always　(部分否定：必ずしも〜でない)

    ex 4) Dreams <u>don't always</u> come true. (本文第 1 段落)

no longer　(もはや〜ではない)

=not any longer

    ex 5) They <u>no longer</u> share the same interests. (本文第 3 段落)
       =They <u>don't</u> share the same interests <u>any longer</u>. /They <u>don't any longer</u>
       share the same interest.

✎ Grammar Practice

次の日本語文に合うように英語文を完成させましょう。ただし文頭に来る語も小文字にしてあります。

1. その子どもたちには外に出て遊ぶ時間がありませんでした。

   [didn't / and play / the children / go / time / outdoors / to / have].

   _____

2. 彼らは数学やコンピュータ技術が得意ではありません。

   [good / math / they / technology / or / at / aren't / computer].

   _____

3. 私の娘はあのおもちゃにはもはや興味がありません。

[in / longer / is / my daughter / toy / interested / that / no].

_____

4. お金がないのならアルバイトを探すべきです。

[should / a part-time job / you / if / money / find / no / you have].

_____

6 Dialogue 🎧 29

音声を聞いて、日本語を参考にしながら空欄に聞き取った英語を書きましょう。

Toshiko shares some shocking news about her parents with her American friend Jimmy.

Toshiko: Oh, Jimmy! You _____. My parents
(何が起こったか信じられないでしょう)
are getting divorced after 30 years of marriage!

Jimmy: I'm so sorry, Toshiko, but these things happen. Nowadays
_____ are getting divorced.
(さらに多くの年配の夫婦が)

Toshiko: But why? I mean, after 30 years of marriage, can't they work
something out?

Jimmy: Easier said than done. During their marriage, they've probably
grown apart – your father always in the office and your mother
always at home.

Toshiko: So you're telling me that they're like strangers to each other, and
they don't want to spend time together.

Jimmy: Precisely! So in these cases, divorce is probably the best solution,
_____ it.
(彼らに金銭的余裕がある限りは)

🌐 **Did You Know?**

アメリカの離婚率は高いイメージがありますが、世界で最も離婚する国というわけではありません。例えば、ヨーロッパには、アメリカの離婚率より高い国が多くあります。アメリカの初婚率は大体45％であり、再婚や再々婚よりも高くなっています。また、近年では、アメリカの離婚率は減少してきています。単純に、結婚するアメリカ人が少なくなってきていることが原因でもありますが、金銭的な問題など、結婚願望があるのにできない人が増えてきていることも原因のようです。

7 Now It's Your Turn!

次の３つのトピックから１つ選び、回答例や Useful Expressions を参考にしながらパートナーと話し合ってみましょう。準備として、自分の意見をまとめておくと話し合いやすくなります。

1. Do you approve or disapprove of silver divorces?   Please explain your answer.
2. Discuss the reasons why silver divorces don't always work out well.
3. Discuss the reasons why silver divorces often work out well.

番号： ☐

自分の意見 ....

....

....

回答例

1. I don't approve of silver divorces. After many years of marriage, couples should work out their problems. And silver divorces aren't good for the kids and grandkids.

2. Well, some people just don't adjust well to change. If they don't make new friends and get new interests, they may feel depressed.

3. Some people finally have the chance to do what they've always wanted to do – travel, go back to school, start a new career.

Useful Expressions

- I approve of silver divorces because ...: 熟年離婚はよいと思います。なぜなら～
- After many years of marriage, couples should ...: 長年にわたる結婚生活を経て、夫婦は～すべきです。
- Silver divorces aren't good for ...: 熟年離婚は～にとってよくありません。
- There's the question of money.: お金の問題があります。
- Remarrying is great as long as ...: 再婚は～であるかぎりよいことです。

Chapter 8 — Trees: A Gift from Nature

森林伐採の問題は、多くのメディアで取りあげられ、我々が対処しなければならない重要な問題です。では、なぜ我々は、「木」を大切にしなければならないのでしょうか？

本章では、「木」を守る意義を考えてみましょう。また、私たち個人ができることは何でしょうか？

① Pre-Reading Questions 30

以下のイラストを参考にして、英文の下線部の意味を枠内の選択肢より選んで記号（a 〜 f）で答えましょう。

| 1 strong winds | 2 heavy rain | 3 insects |
| 4 lightning | 5 factories | 6 erosion |

1. **Strong winds** can cause flight delays.　　　　　　　　[　　]
2. **Heavy rain** often causes flooding.　　　　　　　　　　[　　]
3. Butterflies are beautiful **insects**.　　　　　　　　　　[　　]
4. **Lightning** is dangerous because it causes wildfires and even kills people.

　　　　　　　　　　　　　　　　　　　　　　　　　　　[　　]
5. **Factories** sometimes pollute the environment.　　　　[　　]
6. Trees protect the ground from **erosion**.　　　　　　　[　　]

| a) 大雨 | b) 昆虫 | c) 強風 |
| d) 稲妻、雷 | e) 浸食 | f) 工場 |

Trees are a special gift from nature.
Sometimes people forget all the wonderful things
they do for us. They protect us from the hot sun,
strong winds and heavy rain. They give us delicious fruits and nuts. They are
5 beautiful to look at, especially in the spring and fall.

Trees also help the environment. In addition to cleaning and cooling the
air, they protect the ground from erosion. Birds, small animals and insects
build nests in trees for safety and protection from bad weather.

Unfortunately trees are in danger from both natural and human causes.
10 Some die from diseases, while others are destroyed by wildfires or lightning.
Too many are cut down to make open space for new homes, factories and
farms.

To stop this danger, we must plant more trees – in the country, in the
suburbs and especially in the cities. According to researchers, trees improve
15 the quality of city life. Since more and more people are living in cities, the
green spaces must be increased.

Many cities have ambitious plans. They are planting trees on sidewalks,
in malls and around offices and apartment buildings. They are creating *urban
forests* – that is, areas with lots of trees. Here people can walk, exercise, or
20 simply relax and enjoy the peace and beauty of nature.

These urban forests also protect the environment. They lower the
temperature of the air in the summer so people need less AC. In this way, trees
help reduce energy use. The air is cleaner because trees absorb carbon dioxide.
Thanks to these urban forests, many birds, bees, butterflies and small animals
25 are coming back to the cities.

To protect trees is a way to thank nature for this special gift.

(Words: 284)

Notes
| nuts: ナッツ、木の実
| nests: 巣
| green spaces: 緑地
| urban forests: 都市林

AC: = air conditioning
absorb: 吸収する
carbon dioxide: 二酸化炭素

③ Comprehension Questions

本文の内容に合っている文には T を、合っていない文には F を [   ] に記入しましょう。

1. Trees do many special things for people and also for the environment.

   [   ]

2. Trees are in danger only because of natural causes such as wildfires or diseases.   [   ]

3. Many cities are planting trees because green spaces improve the quality of city life.   [   ]

4. Urban forests provide a home for birds, bees, butterflies and small animals.

   [   ]

④ Guided Summary   CD 32

次の英文は本文を要約したものです。(1) から (8) の空所に、下の (a) 〜 (h) から適語を選んで記入し文を完成させましょう。

Trees are a special gift from nature. They do many (1)_____ things for us, and they also (2)_____ the environment. Unfortunately trees are in (3)_____ from both natural and human causes. That's why it's important to (4)_____ more trees. Many cities have plans to (5)_____ urban (6)_____ — that is, green spaces with lots of trees. These urban forests improve the (7)_____ of city life, and also protect the (8)_____.

📓 Word List

(a) forests	**(b)** environment	**(c)** protect	**(d)** quality
(e) create	**(f)** wonderful	**(g)** plant	**(h)** danger

⑤ Essential Grammar   不定詞

「to ＋動詞の原形」の形を不定詞と呼び、次のような用法があります。

▌名詞用法

「〜すること」と訳され、不定詞が文の主語、目的語、補語になります。

ex 1) To protect trees is a way to thank nature for this special gift. (本文第 7 段落)
　　　to protect trees が文の主語になっています。⇒「木々を守ること」が〜

▌形容詞用法

「〜すべき」「〜するための」と名詞を修飾する用法です。

ex 2) Death was the only way to be together. (Chapter 5 本文第 3 段落)
　　　名詞 way(方法) を不定詞 to be 以下が修飾しています。⇒「一緒になるための」方法

ex 1) の a way to thank nature も不定詞の形容詞的用法です。⇒「自然に感謝するための」
　　　　　　　　　　　　　　　　　　　　　　　　　　　　　　　　　　方法

▌副詞用法

「〜するために」「〜して」と動詞や形容詞等を修飾する方法です。

ex 3) Too many are cut down to make open space for new homes. (本文第 3 段落)
　　　to make が動詞句 are cut down を修飾している副詞用法です。

ex 4) To stop this danger, we must plant more trees. (本文第 4 段落目)
　　　to stop が動詞句 must plant more trees を修飾しています。⇒「この危険状態を止め
　　　るために」植えなくてはならない

✎ Grammar Practice

次の日本語文に合うように英語文を完成させましょう。ただし文頭に来る語も小文字にしてあ
ります。

1. 私の兄はそのサッカークラブに参加したがっています。

   [club / my / join / wants / older / the soccer / to / brother].

   _____

2. 多くの人々が美しい桜を見るために日本を訪れます。

   [come / cherry blossoms / view / to / many people / to / beautiful / Japan].

   _____

3. 彼女が帰国すると聞いて、私はとても悲しいです。

   [very sad / going / hear / I'm / her country / that / to / she's / back to].

   _____

4. 何か飲み物を持ってきましょうか？

[may / bring / anything / I / drink / to / you]?

_____

6 Dialogue 🎵 33

音声を聞いて、日本語を参考にしながら空欄に聞き取った英語を書きましょう。

Junko is talking with her American friend Fred, who has been working in Tokyo for about six months.

Junko: Fred, you've been in Tokyo for about six months. How do you like living here?

Fred: Now I really like Tokyo, but at first it wasn't easy adjusting to a new lifestyle.

Junko: Of course, a new city, a new language and new friends – that's not

_____!
（簡単なもの）

Fred: And you've gotta remember that I'm a country boy, so city life was a big change – so much noise, so many people, and so much to do.

Junko: What made you change your mind about city life?

Fred: The great parks in Tokyo! When I'm tired of city life, I just

_____ and connect with nature.
（そこに行ってリラックスする）

Junko: So now you have _____!
（両方のいいところ）

🌐 **Did You Know?**

「樹木」には特別な意味があるのを知っていますか？　オークの木は「勇気」や「強さ」のシンボルであり、オリーブの木は「平和」や「友情」を表します。常緑樹は、常に緑であることから「永遠の命」を表し、日本の桜の木は、「美」や「純潔さ」を我々に思い出させてくれます。木の持ついろいろな意味を調べてみるのも面白いですね。

7 Now It's Your Turn!

次の３つのトピックから１つ選び、回答例や Useful Expressions を参考にしながらパートナーと話し合ってみましょう。準備として、自分の意見をまとめておくと話し合いやすくなります。

1. Why are urban forests important for cities?
2. Why are trees in danger today?
3. Do you think that it's better to live in a city or in the country?

番号：☐

自分の意見 ....

....

....

回答例

1. Urban forests improve the quality of city life. In these green spaces, people can relax and connect with nature.

2. Many trees are destroyed by natural causes such as wildfires or lightning. Some trees die from diseases.

3. For me, city life is better, especially if you're young and single. It's fun, exciting, and you get to meet cool people from all over the world.

Useful Expressions

- Urban forests improve the quality of city life.: 都市林は都市生活の質を向上させます。
- Urban forests help protect the environment.: 都市林は環境を守るのに役立ちます。
- Many trees are destroyed by ...: 多くの木が〜によって破壊されています。
- For me, city life is better because ...: 私にとっては、都市部での生活の方がいいです。なぜなら〜

Chapter 9 Tattoos

　欧米では、「タトゥー」はファッションの一部として認識され、特に若い世代に普及しています。世界各国で、タトゥーに対する認識は異なり、日本においては広く普及しているとは言えません。

　あなたはファッションとしてのタトゥーに賛成ですか？　それとも反対ですか？

① Pre-Reading Questions 🎧 34

以下のイラストを参考にして、英文の下線部の意味を枠内の選択肢より選んで記号（a ～ f）で答えましょう。

| 1 statistics | 2 taboo | 3 cosmetic |
| 4 athletes | 5 dislike | 6 painful |

1. <u>Statistics</u> often give us interesting information.　　[　　]
2. A <u>taboo</u> is something you can't do or say.　　[　　]
3. She took a job in the <u>cosmetic</u> industry.　　[　　]
4. <u>Athletes</u> from all over the world compete in the Olympics.　　[　　]
5. I really <u>dislike</u> rush hour in Tokyo.　　[　　]
6. Getting an injection is sometimes <u>painful</u>.　　[　　]

| **a)** 美容の、化粧用の | **b)** 運動選手 | **c)** 統計 |
| **d)** 嫌う | **e)** 禁止、禁句 | **f)** 苦痛な |

2 Reading Passage

 35

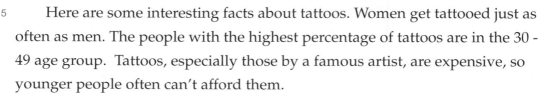

Today tattoos have gone mainstream. According to some recent statistics, one out of every three Americans has a tattoo. Tattoos are also popular in Australia, Canada and various European nations. Fifty years ago, however, tattoos were taboo!

5 Here are some interesting facts about tattoos. Women get tattooed just as often as men. The people with the highest percentage of tattoos are in the 30 - 49 age group. Tattoos, especially those by a famous artist, are expensive, so younger people often can't afford them.

Why do some people like tattoos? First of all, they think tattoos are trendy
10 because they are so popular with movie stars and athletes. Tattoos let people express their personality since they choose the designs that they like. For them, tattoos are beautiful body art.

The so-called cosmetic tattoos are popular among women who want permanent makeup on their brows, eyes or lips. This solution is convenient
15 because they no longer have to worry about makeup.

Why do some people dislike tattoos? In their opinion, tattoos are unattractive. Worse still, they often look bad as people age, or gain or lose weight.

There are also health risks such as infection or allergic reactions, especially
20 for cosmetic tattoos on the eyelids. It's very painful and expensive to remove tattoos if you don't like them anymore.

Last but not least, tattoos – especially on the neck, face or hands – can hurt a person's job chances. Many professions such as banking, law or healthcare generally don't hire individuals with tattoos that can be seen.

25 Tattoos send a message. Depending on your point of view, the message can be positive or negative. What's your opinion?

(Words: 274)

Notes

get tattooed: タトゥーを入れる	**allergic reaction:** アレルギー反応
brow: 眉	**eyelid:** まぶた
unattractive: 魅力のない、つまらない	**healthcare:** 医療

③ Comprehension Questions

本文の内容に合っている文には T を、合っていない文には F を ［　　］ に記入しましょう。

1. The people with the highest percentage of tattoos are women in the 30 – 49 age group.　　　　　　　　　　　　　　　　　　　　　［　　］

2. Everybody agrees that tattoos are beautiful body art.　　　［　　］

3. Cosmetic tattoos are convenient, but sometimes can cause infection or allergic reactions.　　　　　　　　　　　　　　　　　　　［　　］

4. If you have tattoos on your neck, face or hands, you may have problems finding a job.　　　　　　　　　　　　　　　　　　　　　［　　］

④ Guided Summary　　🎧 36

次の英文は本文を要約したものです。(1) から (8) の空所に、下の (a) ～ (h) から適語を選んで記入し文を完成させましょう。

Today in many countries, tattoos have gone (1)＿＿＿＿＿＿. Women get tattooed just as often as men. Individuals in the 30-49 age group have the highest (2)＿＿＿＿＿ of tattoos. Some people like tattoos because they are (3)＿＿＿＿＿. They also let you express your (4)＿＿＿＿＿ because you choose the design. Cosmetic tattoos are popular among women who want (5)＿＿＿＿＿ makeup. Other people, however, think that tattoos are ugly. (6)＿＿＿＿＿ them is painful and (7)＿＿＿＿＿. Sometimes tattoos can hurt your (8)＿＿＿＿＿ chances.

📓 Word List

(a) personality	**(b)** mainstream	**(c)** job	**(d)** removing
(e) percentage	**(f)** expensive	**(g)** trendy	**(h)** permanent

5 Essential Grammar 　前置詞

名詞や代名詞の前に置き、他の語との関係を表す語が前置詞です。

about 　(〜について、〜に関する)

about tattoos (第2段落), about makeup (第4段落)

among 　(〜の間で、〜の中で)

among women (第4段落)

as 　(〜として、〜のような)

as models (Chapter 4 本文第4段落)
such as infection(第6段落), such as banking(第7段落) のように例を示す時に、such as の形でよく使われる。

by 　(〜による、〜のそばに)

by a famous artist (第2段落), side by side (Chapter 5 本文第4段落)

for 　(〜にとって、〜のために、〜の間)

for cosmetic tattoos (第6段落), for this reason (Chapter 1 本文第2段落), for more than 75 years (Chapter 1 本文第1段落)

in 　(〜の中に)

in Australia (第1段落), in the 30-49 age group (第2段落)

of 　(〜の、〜の中で)

percentage of tattoos (第2段落), point of view (第8段落), first of all (第3段落)

on 　(〜の上に、〜について、〜に頼って)

on their brows (第4段落), on the eyelids (第6段落), on the neck (第7段落), focus on the workplace (Chapter 3 本文第2段落), depending on (第8段落)

with 　(〜と、〜とともに、〜のある)

with movie stars (第3段落), individuals with tattoos (第7段落)

Grammar Practice

次の日本語文に合うように英語文を完成させましょう。ただし文頭に来る語も小文字にしてあります。

1. 学生の5人に1人がその試験をパスすることができませんでした。

   [every / couldn't / one / five students / pass / out / the exam / of].

   _____

2. イングランド、オーストラリア、インドなど、多くの国々でクリケットは人気があります。

   [England, Australia and India / popular / cricket / such / many countries / as / in / is].

   _____

3. ハローキティは世界中の女の子に人気があります。

   [the world / Hello Kitty / over / popular / is / all / among / girls].

   _____

4. 結果はあなたの努力次第です。

   [depend / the / efforts / on / result / will / your].

   _____

6 Dialogue 37

音声を聞いて、日本語を参考にしながら空欄に聞き取った英語を書きましょう。

Linda is asking her Japanese friend Yasushi for advice.

Linda: Oh, Yasushi, I'm SO upset with my sister. I just don't know what to do.

Yasushi: Calm down, Linda, and just tell me what happened.

Linda: She – she wants to get a tattoo! _____?
（彼女はいったいどうしたんだ）

What should I tell her?

Yasushi: Well, _____ that getting tattooed hurts.
（彼女に気づかせた方がいいよ）

It's also very expensive and painful to remove these tattoos.

Linda: And tattoos are so ugly. Many companies won't hire people with tattoos.

Yasushi: So just _____ why this isn't a good
（落ち着いて〜について彼女に話す）

idea.

Linda: Oh, Yasushi, thanks so much for your help.

Did You Know?

ポリネシアへの航海からイングランドに帰国したキャプテン・クックは、タヒチの人々が美しいボディーアートをしていたことを話しました。これらのボディーアートを施した人は、鋭利な道具で肌を刺し（hit the skin）、インクをすり込んだといいます。英語の tattoo はポリネシアの言葉の tautau（指すという意味）に由来しています。この言葉を英語にもたらしたキャプテン・クックに我々は感謝しなければなりませんね。

7 Now It's Your Turn!

次の 3 つのトピックから 1 つ選び、回答例や Useful Expressions を参考にしながらパートナーと話し合ってみましょう。準備として、自分の意見をまとめておくと話し合いやすくなります。

1. Do you like/dislike tattoos? Explain your answer.
2. Discuss some of the disadvantages of tattoos.
3. Discuss the pros and cons of cosmetic tattoos.

番号： ☐

自分の意見

....

....

....

回答例

1. Well, I think they're trendy. Nowadays tattoos have gone mainstream. It's not like in the past when they were taboo.

2. Well, first of all, you might not get hired if you have tattoos on your neck, face or hands. Then there are health risks – infection or allergic reactions.

3. They're great for girls who don't like putting on makeup every day. But sometimes cosmetic tattoos cause infection or allergic reactions.

Useful Expressions

- I think they're trendy.: 私はそれらはおしゃれだと思います。
- You might not get hired if you have tattoos.: もしあなたにタトゥーがあれば、雇用されないかもしれません。
- There are health risks such as ...: 〜といった健康上のリスクがあります。
- They're great for girls who ...: 〜な女性には、それらはすばらしいです。

Chapter 10
Redefining Gender and Marriage

多様性が注目されるようになり、「性別」と「結婚」の定義も変化してきています。そういった変化に伴い、言語も変化しています。

　本章では、社会の変化が言語にどのような変化をもたらすのか考えてみましょう。

① Pre-Reading Questions 38

以下のイラストを参考にして、英文の下線部の意味を枠内の選択肢より選んで記号（a 〜 f）で答えましょう。

1 social customs	2 refer to	3 application
4 passport	5 comfortable	6 tradition

1. The <u>social customs</u> in Saudi Arabia are very different from those in Canada. [　　]

2. The chairperson <u>referred to</u> the committee report during the meeting. [　　]

3. This job <u>application</u> is so long – over 15 pages. [　　]

4. You need a <u>passport</u> for international travel. [　　]

5. When I travel, I always wear <u>comfortable</u> clothes. [　　]

6. The tea ceremony is an important Japanese <u>tradition</u>. [　　]

a) 心地よい	b) 社会的習慣	c) 〜に言及する
d) 旅券	e) 願書	f) 伝統

Language is a mirror of society, and changes as social customs change. That is why words often need new definitions. Today we will look at two examples in English.

Let's start with the word *gender*, which traditionally refers to either *males*
5 or *females*. For some people, especially in the homosexual community, these two choices are not enough. They insist that there should also be a third choice for individuals who do not identify themselves as either male or female. They suggest using the letter *X* to indicate a third gender.

Recently in the US, many applications for jobs, school admission and
10 official documents offer three choices: $M - F - X$. The US and some European countries now issue *X passports* – that is, passports with three options for gender.

Let's move on to *marriage*, which has been traditionally defined as the legal union between a man and a woman. In recent years, however, many
15 countries have legalized same-sex marriage. Now English dictionaries define marriage as the legal union between two people.

The new definition of marriage creates problems about how to describe a married couple. Traditionally the *husband* is a man, and the *wife* is a woman, but this is not the case in same-sex marriages. Some people prefer to use *spouse*
20 because this word refers to both men and women.

Not everybody, however, feels comfortable with the new definitions of gender and marriage because change is a threat to tradition. People who like tradition dislike change. Those who dislike tradition like change.

What is your opinion about these new definitions of gender and marriage?

(Words: 263)

③ Comprehension Questions

本文の内容に合っている文には T を、合っていない文には F を ［　］に記入しましょう。

1. Words need new definitions when social customs change.　　　　［　　］
2. Everybody agrees that there are only two genders.　　　　　　　［　　］
3. In countries where same-sex marriage is legal, marriage is now defined as the union between two people rather than the union between a man and a woman.　　　　　　　　　　　　　　　　　　　　　　　　　　　［　　］
4. Some people dislike change because it's a threat to tradition.　　［　　］

④ Guided Summary　🎧 40

次の英文は本文を要約したものです。(1) から (8) の空所に、下の (a) 〜 (h) から適語を選んで記入し文を完成させましょう。

Language changes as social (1)＿＿＿＿＿＿ change, so words often need new
(2)＿＿＿＿＿＿ . Traditionally (3)＿＿＿＿＿＿ referred to males and females.
Now some people want a third choice for (4)＿＿＿＿＿＿ who do not
(5)＿＿＿＿＿＿ themselves as either male or female. Marriage used to be
the legal (6)＿＿＿＿＿＿ between a man and a woman. In countries where
same-sex marriage is legal, the definition has been (7)＿＿＿＿＿＿ to the
union between two people. For some, these changes are a (8)＿＿＿＿＿＿ to
tradition.

🗒 Word List

(a) gender　　　(b) union　　　(c) customs　　　(d) threat
(e) changed　　(f) definitions　(g) identify　　 (h) individuals

⑤ Essential Grammar 〔現在完了形〕

現在完了は、「have [has] ＋過去分詞」という形で、「完了」「結果」「経験」「継続」などの意味を表します。過去の出来事が何らかの形で現在に影響を与えているというニュアンスを表しています。

現在完了形が表す意味

①完了「もう～してしまった」「今～したところだ」など、現在までに動作が完了したことを表す。

ex 1) The train has just left. (電車は今出たところです)

②結果「～している」「～して今は…だ」など、過去の動作の後の、現在における結果を表す。

ex 2) Many countries have legalized same-sex marriage. (本文第4段落)
ex 3) They have fallen out of love. (Chapter 7 本文第3段落)

③経験「これまでに～したことがある」など現在までの経験を表す。

ex 4) I've never heard of that. (Chapter 4 Dialogue)

④継続「～している」など過去から現在までの継続を表す。

ex 5) Marriage has been traditionally defined as the legal union between a man and a woman. (本文第4段落)

   この文は、「have been ＋過去分詞」と受動態の現在完了形の文になっています。

ex 6) Magazines have shown pictures of these perfect women. (Chapter 4 本文第2段落)
ex 7) You've been in Tokyo for about six months. (Chapter 8 Dialogue)

✎ Grammar Practice

次の日本語文に合うように英語文を完成させましょう。ただし文頭に来る語も小文字にしてあります。

1. 政府はギャンブルを合法化しました。

   [legalized / the / gambling / has / government].

   _____

2. その椅子は20年間使われていますが、新品に見えます。

   [20 years / has / the chair / looks new / used / been / but it / for].

   _____

3. 私は3回オーストラリアに行ったことがあります。

   [three / I / to / have / Australia / been / times].

   _____

4. 私の友だちの何人かはすでに帰宅しました。

[of / home / already / gone / some / friends / my / have].

_____

6 Dialogue 🎵 41

音声を聞いて、日本語を参考にしながら空欄に聞き取った英語を書きましょう。

Mariko is studying psychology at an American university. She is going to have coffee with her American friend Ken.

Ken: Hey, Mariko! Great to see you. Everything's _____
　　　　　　　　　　　　　　　　　　　　　　　　　　　　（うまくいってる）

　　　　　_____ ?

Mariko: Yeah! I really like all my classes, especially the psych course. We're
　　　　　studying some really challenging topics.

Ken: Like what?

Mariko: Like marriage is no longer the union between a man and a woman.
　　　　　In some countries, same-sex marriage is now legal.

Ken: Seems _____, but I'm sure that not everybody is
　　　　　　　　　（僕にとっては公正なこと）

　　　　　happy with this change.

Mariko: So right you are. Some people think that change is a threat to
　　　　　tradition. And they don't like that.

Ken: OK, but change can also _____ for the future!
　　　　　　　　　　　　　　　　　　　（物事をよりよくする）

Note | psych: = psychology 心理学

🌐 Did You Know?

自分の性を「男性」とも「女性」とも認識しない人は、自身の性を「第3の性」と自認します。理由としては、性には3つの選択肢があることを知ってもらいたいことが挙げられます（M：男性、F：女性、X：男性・女性どちらにもあてはまらない）。今日、いくつかの国では「Xパスポート」が発行されています。パスポートの性別欄には「X」と記載されています。また、ネパールでは性別欄に「O」（other）と記載されたパスポートを発行しています。

7 Now It's Your Turn!

次の３つのトピックから１つ選び、回答例や Useful Expressions を参考にしながらパートナーと話し合ってみましょう。準備として、自分の意見をまとめておくと話し合いやすくなります。

1. What are the pros and cons of recognizing the third gender?
2. Do you think that change is a threat to tradition?
3. Do you think that the Japanese government should issue X passports?

番号： ☐

自分の意見
_____
_____
_____

回答例

1. It's good to give people who don't identify as either male or female a third choice.

2. Most definitely! Some traditions are OK, but many are old-fashioned. To move forward, we need change.

3. For now, it's not a good idea because some foreign countries don't accept X passports.

Useful Expressions

- It's good to give people who ...: ～という人に与えるのはいいことです。
- It's OK, but not if you ...: もしあなたが～しないならば、いいです。
- To move forward, we need change.: 前に進むには、我々には変化が必要です。
- Change is a threat when it's ...: 変化はそれが～なとき驚異となります。

Chapter 11 *All the Lonely People*

　21世紀の現代において「孤独」は深刻な問題です。ソーシャルメディアの活用が「孤独」を助長しているという指摘もあります。

　本章では、ソーシャルメディアの長所、短所を考え、孤独とどう関わっているのか考えてみましょう。

1 Pre-Reading Questions   42

以下のイラストを参考にして、英文の下線部の意味を枠内の選択肢より選んで記号（a 〜 f）で答えましょう。

1 lonely people	2 social media	3 pros and cons
4 chat	5 video-calling	6 grandchildren

1. Perhaps there are more <u>lonely people</u> today than in the past. [　　]
2. <u>Social media</u> makes it easy to stay in touch with friends and family. [　　]
3. Kiyoshi thought about the <u>pros and cons</u> of renting a car for his trip to Europe. [　　]
4. Today many people like to <u>chat</u> online. [　　]
5. Mariko likes WhatsApp for <u>video-calling</u> because it's free. [　　]
6. <u>Grandchildren</u> can learn a lot from their grandparents. [　　]

a) 賛否両論	b) おしゃべりをする	c) 孫たち
d) 孤独な人々	e) SNS	f) テレビ電話

2 Reading Passage 43

Throughout history, there have always been lonely people. Today, however, the number of lonely individuals seems to be increasing. Some people blame social media, but others disagree. Now let's
5 look at the pros and cons of this problem.

Fans of social media believe that it can help reduce loneliness. It is a fast, easy, and inexpensive way to stay in touch with family and friends. On social networking sites, you can connect with people all over the globe. You can chat with your online friends, and share your opinions. You can get information so
10 you feel involved with what's going on in the world.

Social media is also good for older people, especially if they live far away from family. With video-calling, they can have face-to-face chats with their children and grandchildren. This contact with family makes them feel less lonely.

15 Critics of social media, on the other hand, believe that it can increase loneliness, especially if you spend too much time online. The real danger is not social media in itself but rather how much and how often you use it. Too much time online means too little time in the real world. Don't forget that online friends and online experiences can't replace real-life ones.

20 Spending too much time online is also bad for your health. If you're always checking your phone or computer, you don't have time to hang out with friends, exercise, or sleep. This unhealthy habit can make you feel lonely, tired, and depressed.

Does social media make people more lonely or less lonely? Do you agree
25 with the fans or the critics?

(Words: 267)

③ Comprehension Questions

本文の内容に合っている文には T を、合っていない文には F を ［　］ に記入しましょう。

1. Social media can reduce loneliness because you can stay in touch with family and friends, and you can also chat with online friends. ［　］

2. Social media increases loneliness if you use it too much and too often. ［　］

3. Your online friends and experiences are better than your real-life ones. ［　］

4. Too much time online means too little time for hanging out with friends, exercising and sleeping. ［　］

④ Guided Summary 🎵 44

次の英文は本文を要約したものです。(1) から (8) の空所に、下の (a) 〜 (h) から適語を選んで記入し文を完成させましょう。

Today there are more lonely people than before. Is social media causing this problem? Some say no, and insist that social media (1)＿＿＿＿＿＿ loneliness. After all, social media lets you (2)＿＿＿＿＿ with family and friends, (3)＿＿＿＿＿ with online friends, and get (4)＿＿＿＿＿ with world affairs. But others say that social media can increase (5)＿＿＿＿＿ if you spend too much time (6)＿＿＿＿＿. Let's not forget that social media can't (7)＿＿＿＿＿ real-life friends and (8)＿＿＿＿＿.

📝 Word List

(a) connect　　(b) loneliness　　(c) online　　(d) experiences

(e) replace　　(f) reduces　　(g) chat　　(h) involved

5 Essential Grammar　使役動詞など

本来「使役」というのは「誰かに何かをさせること」ですので、使役動詞というのは「（人）に～させる」という動詞 (make, let, have) になりますが、それに加え help も「（人）を手伝って～させる」という解釈ができるので、ここでは使役動詞と合わせて扱います。
「make/let/have/help ＋人＋動詞の原形（原形不定詞）」の形で使います。

make

「強制的に～させる」という意味です。

ex 1) This contact with family <u>makes</u> them feel less lonely. (本文第 3 段落目)
ex 2) This unhealthy habit can <u>make</u> you feel lonely. (本文第 5 段落)
ex 3) What <u>made</u> you change your mind? (Chapter 8 Dialogue)
　　　Why did you change your mind? ではなく、このように尋ねることも多い。

let

「（相手がしたがっていることを）～させてあげる」という意味です。

ex 4) <u>Let</u> her say what she likes. (彼女には言いたいことを言わせておけ)
ex 5) <u>Let</u> me tell you the truth. (本当のことを言わせてください)

have

「（当然のことを）～させる、～してもらう」という意味です。

ex 6) I will <u>have</u> him wait at the station. (私は駅で彼を待たせておきます)

help

「（人を手伝って）～させる」「人が～するのを手伝う」という意味です。

ex 7) I <u>helped</u> him study English. (私は彼が英語を勉強するのを手伝いました)
ex 8) Social media can <u>help</u> reduce loneliness. (本文第 2 段落)
　　　「help + to 不定詞」形もあるが、「help ＋原形不定詞」がしばしば用いられる。

Grammar Practice

次の日本語文に合うように英語文を完成させましょう。ただし文頭に来る語も小文字にしてあります。

1. さあ、まずはメニューを見てみよう。

   [look / now, / first / at / let's / menu / the].

   _____

2. このかわいらしいマスコットはあなたを幸せな気持ちにしてくれます。

   [mascot / make / this / feel / can / cute / you / happy].

   _____

3. 私の上司はケンにプロジェクトの進捗状況を報告させました。

[my / progress / boss / had / the / report / Ken / project's].

_____

4. もし質問があれば、私に知らせてください。

[you / me / know / please / any questions / let / have / if].

_____

6 Dialogue 🎧 45

音声を聞いて、日本語を参考にしながら空欄に聞き取った英語を書きましょう。

Masato is chatting with his friend Nancy, an American exchange student in Tokyo.

Masato: Hey, Nancy? _____? You look really happy.
（どうしたんだい）

Nancy: Yes, I am. I just did FaceTime with my folks.

Masato: I bet you'd feel lonely if _____ them.
（あなたが〜とおしゃべりしなかった）

Nancy: You're so right. Social media is really great. It keeps us all connected, so we don't feel lonely.

Masato: Well, not always because some people – like my roommate – are lonely because they _____ online.
（多くの時間を費やす）

Nancy: That happens, and isn't good. You've gotta find a happy medium.

Masato: I agree 100 percent.

Notes | **folks:** 家族、人々　**bet:** きっと〜に違いない　**happy medium:** 折衷案、妥協点

🌐 **Did You Know?**

いくつかの研究では、スマートフォンやタブレットを過剰に利用すると、憂鬱な気分を助長し、自殺まで引き起こす可能性があると指摘しています。就寝前のベッドでの使用を避け、ゲームなどの娯楽での使用は１日２時間までにするべきと主張する専門家もいます。「スマホ依存」という言葉もよく聞かれるようになり、スマホの過剰利用と脳との関係も指摘されています。節度を守り、快適に利用する習慣をつけることが重要です。

7 Now It's Your Turn!

次の３つのトピックから１つ選び、回答例や Useful Expressions を参考にしながらパートナーと話し合ってみましょう。準備として、自分の意見をまとめておくと話し合いやすくなります。

1. Some people believe that social media reduces loneliness. Do you agree? Explain your answer.

2. Some people believe that social media increases loneliness. Do you agree? Explain your answer.

3. Discuss how social media can affect your health.

番号：
自分の意見

回答例

1. I agree. Social media reduces loneliness because we can stay in touch with family and friends. It's also great for older people.

2. I agree that it increases loneliness because you can get addicted to social media. Online experiences can't replace real-life ones.

3. Too much time online means too little or no time in the real world. Unhealthy habits can make you feel sick and lonely.

Useful Expressions

- Connecting with family and friends is good.: 家族や友だちとつながっていることはいいことです。
- With social media, you can ...: ソーシャルメディアを使えば、あなたは〜ができます。
- You can get addicted to social media.: あなたは、ソーシャルメディアの依存症になる可能性があります。
- Unhealthy habits can make you feel ...: 不健康な習慣はあなたを〜な気分にさせる可能性があります。
- If you don't sleep enough, you'll be ...: 十分な睡眠がとれなければ、あなたは〜になるでしょう。

Chapter 12
Think Before You Talk, Text, or Tweet

SNSの手軽さから、多くの人が自分の意見を発信しています。一度「送信ボタン」を押すと、あなたの発信は多くの人が目にすることができ、そして拡散します。

思いついたことをすぐに発信するのではなく、発信する前に一度、その内容について考えてみることが必要かもしれません。

1 Pre-Reading Questions 46

以下のイラストを参考にして、英文の下線部の意味を枠内の選択肢より選んで記号（a ～ f）で答えましょう。

1 wise	**2** regret	**3** tweets
4 grammar	**5** body language	**6** commute

1. He always makes <u>wise</u> choices for his children. [   ]
2. Tom <u>regrets</u> his decision not to get his college degree. [   ]
3. Some students send <u>tweets</u> during class. [   ]
4. For many foreigners, Japanese <u>grammar</u> is very difficult. [   ]
5. <u>Body language</u> in Japan is very different from body language in Italy.

   [   ]
6. I start work at 10:00 am, so I don't <u>commute</u> during rush hour. [   ]

---

a) 賢い   **b)** ツイッターへの投稿   **c)** 身振り手ぶり

d) 通勤する   **e)** 文法   **f)** 後悔する

My grandmother was a wise woman who gave me lots of good advice. One of the most important lessons I learned from her was *Think Before You Speak!* She told me that I should always *Count to Ten* before I talked. In this way, I wouldn't
5 say something that I would later regret.

Since then, the world has changed greatly, but my grandmother's advice is still valid – maybe even more so because of the Internet. Today we "speak" to each other with emails, texts or tweets. But this communication is not really "speech" since it is written rather than spoken. What does this mean?

10 I like to refer to this new combination of writing and speaking as *written speech*. When we text, tweet, or email, we write the way we speak – that is, we use slang, abbreviations and informal grammar. But these messages do not express the emotions or body language of a real-life conversation. To let the reader "see" our feelings, we need to add *emoji* to our messages.

15 This new style of communication is convenient, fast and silent, so we can send our messages when we commute, when we are eating, and even when we are in class. But remember that messages on the Internet can never be erased. An old proverb reminds us that spoken words fly away, but written ones remain.

20 Now you know why it's important to think before you talk, text, or tweet. Are you going to take my grandmother's advice and count to ten before you talk, text, or tweet?

(Words: 257)

Notes | **valid:** 有効な、もっともな
slang: スラング、俗語

abbreviation: 短縮、略語
emoji: 絵文字

③ Comprehension Questions

本文の内容に合っている文には T を、合っていない文には F を [   ] に記入しましょう。

1. If you count to ten before you speak, you'll say something you'll later regret. [   ]
2. When we email or text, we usually write the way we speak. [   ]
3. People often add emoji to express emotions in their messages. [   ]
4. Emails, texts and tweets are convenient and safe because they can easily be erased. [   ]

④ Guided Summary 🎧 48

次の英文は本文を要約したものです。(1) から (8) の空所に、下の (a) ～ (h) から適語を選んで記入し文を完成させましょう。

You should (1)＿＿＿＿＿ to count to ten before you speak so that you won't say something you'll later (2)＿＿＿＿＿. Today this (3)＿＿＿＿＿ is more important than ever because people "speak" to each other when they email, text, or tweet – that is, they write the way they speak. Some even add emoji to (4)＿＿＿＿＿ their emotions. This new style of communication is (5)＿＿＿＿＿ and fast but (6)＿＿＿＿＿ because these messages can never be (7)＿＿＿＿＿. That's why it's wise to (8)＿＿＿＿＿ to ten before you talk, text, or tweet.

📝 Word List

| (a) express | (b) advice | (c) count | (d) dangerous |
| (e) remember | (f) erased | (g) convenient | (h) regret |

⑤ Essential Grammar　　受動態

能動態の文型の目的語を主語にして「〜は…される」という文型で同じ内容を表すと、それを受動態といいます。

能動態

受動態

現在形の受動態

ex 1) This communication is written. (本文第 2 段落)
　　時制が is で現在形になっています。一般的な内容なので、一般の人々を表す by us (私たちによって) が省略されています。

過去形の受動態

ex 2) This letter was written by my grandfather. (この手紙は私の祖父によって書かれました)
　　時制が was で過去形になっています。

未来形の受動態

ex 3) The author's new book will be published soon. (その著者の新著は間もなく出版されます)
　　時制が will be で未来形になっています。出版社によって出版されることは、明らかでありあまり重要ではないので by 〜は省略されています。

✏ Grammar Practice

次の日本語文に合うように英語文を完成させましょう。ただし文頭に来る語も小文字にしてあります。

1. その教科書は英語のみで書かれています。

   [only / textbook / written / the / in / English / is].

   _____

2. 彼の意思は決して崩れません。[be / can / his / broken / never / will].

   _____

3. その犬は、先月、消防士たちによって助けられました。

   [last / the / firefighters / dog / by / rescued / was / month].

   _____

4. あなたのおかけになった番号は変更されました。

[changed / number / called / been / the / you / has / have].

_____

6 Dialogue 49

音声を聞いて、日本語を参考にしながら空欄に聞き取った英語を書きましょう。

Cathy is really angry because her boyfriend just broke up with her. She's telling her friend Yoshi what happened.

Cathy: Oh, Yoshi, I'm SO angry at Ralph. I mean, _____

（私たちは付き合っていた）

for over a year and then – out of the blue – he tells me it's over.

Yoshi: _____, Cathy! These things happen all the time. No

（落ち着いて）

point in getting yourself all worked up.

Cathy: Come off it, Yoshi! _____, you'd be

（もしこれがあなたに起こったら）

furious too!

Yoshi: Of course I would, but I'd also move on.

Cathy: Well, before I MOVE ON – as you say – I'm going to email that guy
Ralph, and tell him what I think of him! And it's not going to be nice.

Yoshi: No, Cathy, you're NOT going to send that email. You know that these
things can never be erased.

Cathy: You're right, Yoshi. Sorry that I lost it.

Notes	**out of the blue:** 突然、不意に **Come off it:** やめてよ、まさか	**get all worked up:** 頭に血が上る、興奮する **furious:** 激怒した、逆上した **lost it:** 正気を失なった

Did You Know?

絵文字は今や全世界で使用される「言語」になりました。SNS のメッセージに感情や彩りを加える非常に便利な機能です。絵文字は、日本発祥で世界的に「Emoji」として認識されています。絵文字は世界で最も早く成長した「言語」と言う言語学者もいます。2015 年、オックスフォード英語大辞典が「Emoji」をワード・オブ・ザ・イヤー（流行語大賞）に選びました。

7 Now It's Your Turn!

次の３つのトピックから１つ選び、回答例や Useful Expressions を参考にしながらパートナーと話し合ってみましょう。準備として、自分の意見をまとめておくと話し合いやすくなります。

1. Do you think it's a good idea to count to ten before you talk, text, or tweet?
2. Discuss the pros and cons of written speech.
3. Discuss which is a better communication tool – speaking one-on-one or the written speech of emails, texts and tweets.

番号：

自分の意見

....

....

....

回答例

1. Yes, I do, especially if you're angry or upset. If you don't think, you may say or write something you'll later regret.

2. I think it's great because it lets us "speak" silently to our friends any time and any place.

3. For me, speaking directly is better because you can see my facial expressions and my body language. You can also hear how I change the tone of my voice.

Useful Expressions

- You may say or write something you'll later regret.: 後になって後悔するようなことを言ったり書いたりするかもしれません。
- It's great advice, but ...: それはすばらしいアドバイスですが、～
- I think it's great because ...: それはすばらしいと思います。なぜなら～
- For me, speaking directly is better because ...: 私としては、直接話すほうがいいです。なぜなら～
- For me, both are about the same.: 私としては、両方とも同じです。

Chapter 13 Jeans Go Global!

　インターネットなどの情報通信技術の進展からあらゆる物がグローバル化しています。ニュースなどの情報だけでなく、ファストフード、映画や音楽といった文化、ファッションなども全世界で共有できるようになりました。
　本章では、リーバイスに代表されるジーンズのグローバル化について考えてみましょう。

1 Pre-Reading Questions 🎵 50

以下のイラストを参考にして、英文の下線部の意味を枠内の選択肢より選んで記号（a ～ f）で答えましょう。

| 1 successful | 2 immigrants | 3 clothing store |
| 4 customers | 5 miners | 6 tailor |

1. Amazon is one of the world's most <u>successful</u> companies. [　　]
2. Canada accepts many <u>immigrants</u>. [　　]
3. A boutique is a <u>clothing store</u> that sells expensive clothes. [　　]
4. There are always many <u>customers</u> when there is a sale. [　　]
5. The <u>miners</u> were happy because they discovered gold. [　　]
6. If the sleeves of the jacket are too long, the <u>tailor</u> can shorten them. [　　]

a) 成功した　　　b) 仕立て人　　　c) 鉱夫
d) 洋服店　　　　e) 移民　　　　　f) 客

Jeans are probably the best and most successful example of global fashion. How did this happen?

The story began in 1853 when a German immigrant named Levi Strauss
5 opened a clothing store in San Francisco. Most customers were miners who needed work pants with strong pockets. Jacob Davis, a tailor who worked for Strauss, added copper rivets to strengthen the pockets. These work pants, which were called jeans, quickly became best sellers.

The early jeans were for men only. Farmers, cowboys and construction
10 workers loved them because these pants were comfortable and strong. In those days, the only women who wore jeans were factory workers.

Since 1873, the world has changed a lot, and so have jeans. Today jeans are no longer working pants for men only. Now they are unisex. They come in a huge variety of styles and colors. There are jeans for almost every occasion.
15 You can buy cheap ones in the market or expensive brands by famous designers.

Today jeans have gone global. People wear them at school, at concerts, in restaurants, on planes and trains, and even in church. Many companies have *dress-down Fridays* when employees can wear jeans to work.

20   Not everybody believes that jeans are appropriate for every occasion. They insist that it's important to *dress up* for certain events. In their opinion, *dressing down* is sometimes disrespectful, and shows a lack of good manners, especially in the work place.

Do you like jeans? Do you think that they are OK for every occasion or
25 only for informal ones?

(Words: 256)

Notes

Levi Strauss: リーヴァイ・ストラウス（リーヴァイ・ストラウス社の創業者。1829-1902)
Jacob Davis: ジェイコブ・デイヴィス（仕立て人。衣服にリベットを取り付けることを考案した。1831-1908)
copper rivets: 銅製のリベット（鋲）

1873: ジーンズ誕生の年
unisex: 男女共用の
dress-down Fridays: カジュアルな服装で出勤可能な金曜日
disrespectful: 無礼な
dress up: 着飾る、めかし込む

③ Comprehension Questions

本文の内容に合っている文には T を、合っていない文には F を [　　] に記入しましょう。

1. Levi Strauss's customers wanted strong work pants with no pockets.

[　　]

2. Jacob Davis used copper rivets to strengthen the pockets of the work pants.

[　　]

3. Jeans are popular because they come in many styles and colors.　　[　　]

4. People agree that jeans are appropriate for every occasion.　　[　　]

④ Guided Summary　　🎧 52

次の英文は本文を要約したものです。(1) から (8) の空所に、下の (a) ～ (h) から適語を選んで記入し文を完成させましょう。

In 1853, a German immigrant named Levi Strauss opened a (1)＿＿＿＿＿＿ shop in San Francisco. His (2)＿＿＿＿＿＿ needed strong work pants. A (3)＿＿＿＿＿＿ who worked with Strauss added copper rivets to (4)＿＿＿＿＿＿ the pockets. These work pants were very (5)＿＿＿＿＿＿ and strong. For many years, jeans were only work clothes. Today, however, they are popular with people of all ages, professions and (6)＿＿＿＿＿＿. Today you can choose from a (7)＿＿＿＿＿＿ of styles and colors. Jeans are a (8)＿＿＿＿＿＿ example of global fashion.

📝 Word List

(a) nationalities　　(b) comfortable　　(c) clothing　　(d) successful

(e) customers　　(f) strengthen　　(g) tailor　　(h) variety

5 Essential Grammar 関係代名詞・関係副詞

関係代名詞

人あるいは物が、どのような人かあるいは物かを説明する場合に、関係代名詞 who, which, that などが使われます。

○関係代名詞が、それに続く節の中で主語になる場合 (主格)

ex 1) Most customers were miners who needed strong work pants. (本文第 2 段落)
どんな miners なのかを関係代名詞 who 以下が修飾しています。who は人を表す先行詞を修飾する場合に使われます。

ex 2) I wouldn't say something that I would later regret. (Chapter 12 本文第 1 段落)
先行詞は something(こと) であり、関係代名詞 that が使われ、「私が後で後悔するであろう」が「こと」にかかります。

ex 3) Let's start with the word gender, which traditionally refers to either males or females. (Chapter 10 本文第 2 段落)
関係詞の前にコンマ (,) があるものを非制限用法といいます。「そして、それは〜」のように先行詞を説明します。

関係副詞

関係副詞は、接続詞の働きをするとともに、後ろに続く節に対しては動詞を修飾する副詞の働きをします。時を表す when、場所を表す where、理由を表す why、方法を表す how が主なものです。

ex 4) The story began in 1853 when Levi Strauss opened a clothing store in San Francisco. (本文第 2 段落)
1853 年がどのような時であるかを、when 以下が説明しています。

Grammar Practice

次の日本語文に合うように英語文を完成させましょう。ただし文頭に来る語も小文字にしてあります。

1. ほとんどの客が面接のためにスーツが必要な学生です。

   [are / suits / their job interviews / most customers / who / students / for / need].

   _____

2. 彼女はスポーツカーを 5 台持っている友達がいます。

   [five / who / a friend / has / sports cars / she / has].

   _____

3. 彼は職場での振る舞い方を変えるべきです。

   [the way / should / he / that / at work / behaves / change / he].

   _____

4. 先生の言うことを聞いたらどうですか？

[listen / your teacher / why / you / says / what / to / don't]?

_____

6 Dialogue 🎧 53

音声を聞いて、日本語を参考にしながら空欄に聞き取った英語を書きましょう。

Megan is an American college student. She is talking with Seiichi, an exchange student from Japan, about her new pair of ripped jeans.

Megan: Hey, Seiichi, how do you like my new jeans?

Seiichi: New? They look old to me. They're all ripped and full of holes.

Megan: Oh, Seiichi, you are SO _____. Ripped jeans like these
（時代遅れの）
are really *in* these days.

Seiichi: _____ they're in or out. To me, they just look old
（僕は〜かどうかは気にしない）
and ugly.

Megan: Oh, my God! You're so out of touch with fashion. I mean, do you
even _____ jeans?
（1着持っている）

Seiichi: Of course, I do, but mine look new, and aren't all ripped.

Megan: Seiichi, sometimes you're really impossible!

| **Notes** | ripped: 破れた   **Oh, my God!** は、SNS などで OMG と省略されることがある。 |

 **Did You Know?**

ジーンズ（Jeans）という言葉は、イタリアの都市ジェノバのフランス語標記（Gêne）に由来しています。ジェノバは、船乗りがはくズボンを作るのに必要な良質の綿布を生産していました。また、デニム（Denim）は丈夫な綿布であり、フランス南部の都市ニームで作られていました。フランスの織工はこの綿布を主にイングランドに輸出しており、英語では、de Nîmes（ニーム産）が短縮されて、Denim となりました。

7 Now It's Your Turn!

次の 3 つのトピックから 1 つ選び、回答例や Useful Expressions を参考にしながらパートナーと話し合ってみましょう。準備として、自分の意見をまとめておくと話し合いやすくなります。

1. Why do you like jeans?

2. Is global fashion good or bad?

3. Is it OK to wear jeans to the office?

番号：☐

自分の意見 ....

....

....

回答例

1. I really like jeans because they come in different styles and different colors. They're not expensive, so I can throw away my old jeans, and get a new pair.

2. In my opinion, it's good. When we wear the same fashion, we feel more relaxed, even with people from different countries.

3. No! Jeans are too casual. For the office, you should wear business-style clothes, so you look professional.

Useful Expressions

- I really like jeans because ...: 私はジーンズが本当に好きです。なぜなら〜
- They're not expensive.: それらは高くありません。
- In my opinion, it's good.: 私の意見としては、それはいいことだと思います。
- I don't like global fashion because ...: 私はグローバルファッションは好きではありません。なぜなら〜
- For the office, you should wear ...: オフィスでは、あなたは〜を着るべきです。

Chapter 14
Helping People with Disabilities

　バリアフリー施設は年々増加しており、障害者支援の取り組みは一層広がっています。障害者支援は、社会全体で考えるべき重要な事柄です。

　障害を持つ人のために、我々は今何ができ、また、今後どのように支援していくべきか考えてみましょう。

❶ Pre-Reading Questions　🎧 54

以下のイラストを参考にして、英文の下線部の意味を枠内の選択肢より選んで記号（a ～ f）で答えましょう。

1	2	3
break one's leg	stairs	work together
4	5	6
ramps	handrails	automatic opening doors

1. Hiroki broke his leg when he was playing soccer. 　　　　　　　[　]
2. Climbing stairs is good for your health. 　　　　　　　　　　　[　]
3. When people work together, they can solve problems. 　　　　　[　]
4. Most modern buildings have ramps for people in wheelchairs. 　[　]
5. Handrails on stairways or escalators help prevent people from falling.

　　　　　　　　　　　　　　　　　　　　　　　　　　　　　[　]

6. Automatic opening doors are "user-friendly" for people with disabilities.

　　　　　　　　　　　　　　　　　　　　　　　　　　　　　[　]

a) 協力する	**b)** 手すり	**c)** 階段
d) 自動ドア	**e)** 脚を骨折する	**f)** スロープ

Have you ever broken your leg? If so, you know how difficult daily life becomes. It's painful to walk. Using the stairs is a real challenge, while taking an escalator is very dangerous.

5 People with disabilities face such challenges – and many more – every day. Their disability may be the result of illness, injuries, or age. Their condition limits everyday activities and especially their interaction with the community.

Disability is not only a medical condition. It is also a social problem that affects the lives of the disabled individual, the caregivers and the community.

10 That's why both the government and individuals need to work together to find solutions.

The government has the responsibility to help people with disabilities live better. Public transportation, buildings and schools need to be "user-friendly" for the disabled – more ramps, elevators, handrails, handicap bathrooms,

15 automatic opening doors and sensor lights.

Government guidelines should require hotels to provide more rooms and public facilities for disabled guests. Companies should be encouraged to hire more people with disabilities. Both the public and private sectors need to fund more research on new medications and care robots.

20 At the individual level, we too must do our share. We have to change the way we think about disability and remember that disability does not reduce a person's dignity. We must teach children not to bully or ignore classmates with disabilities. We should do volunteer work.

Helping others, especially people with disabilities, is a positive and

25 powerful way to change society. No matter how small our contribution may be, every little bit counts.

Please think about how you can help people with disabilities.

(Words: 269)

sensor lights: センサーライト（動く物体や その物体の熱量に反応して点灯するライト）

medication: 薬、投薬治療
bully: いじめる

3 Comprehension Questions

本文の内容に合っている文には T を、合っていない文には F を ［　　］ に記入しましょう。

1. Disability is caused only by illness and age. ［　　］
2. Disability is both a medical condition as well as a social problem that affects individuals and the community. ［　　］
3. Governments should be more involved in helping people with disabilities live better. ［　　］
4. Volunteering is the only way to improve the quality of life of people with disabilities. ［　　］

4 Guided Summary 🎧 56

次の英文は本文を要約したものです。(1) から (8) の空所に、下の (a) 〜 (h) から適語を選んで記入し文を完成させましょう。

Disability may be the result of illness, (1)＿＿＿＿＿＿ or age. It is not only a medical condition that (2)＿＿＿＿＿＿ an individual's everyday activities and interaction with the (3)＿＿＿＿＿＿. It is also a social problem that affects the lives of the disabled, the (4)＿＿＿＿＿＿ and society. The government has the (5)＿＿＿＿＿＿ to help people with disabilities live better. As (6)＿＿＿＿＿＿, we too must do our (7)＿＿＿＿＿＿ and remember that disability does not reduce a person's (8)＿＿＿＿＿＿. When we help others, especially people with disabilities, we can change society.

📝 Word List

(a) community　　(b) individuals　　(c) injuries　　(d) responsibility
(e) dignity　　(f) limits　　(g) share　　(h) caregivers

⑤ Essential Grammar 　比較

「A…＋形容詞（または副詞）の比較級＋ than B」または「A…＋ more ＋形容詞（または副詞）＋ than B」で「A は B よりも～だ」という比較の意味を表します。

比較級の作り方と注意点

(i) 一音節の形容詞・副詞の場合は、語尾に -er をつけます。ただし e で終わる語は r だけをつけます。

(ii) more を使うのは、形容詞が二音節の語の一部、三音節以上の時です。

(iii) 不規則変化をする場合もあります。

 ex 1) Playing outdoors makes them physically <u>stronger</u>. (Chapter 6 本文第 3 段落)
  strong に -er をつけて比較級にしています。
 ex 2) A real-life Smokey Bear made the mascot even <u>more famous</u>. (Chapter 1 本文第 4 段落)
  famous は二音節ですが、more をつけて比較級を作る語です。
 ex 3) The government has the responsibility to help people with disabilities live <u>better</u>. (本文第 4 段落)
  better はこの場合は、well の比較級で、不規則変化となります。

(iv) あるものが別のものより程度が低いことを示す劣等比較は「less ＋形容詞 (副詞) の原級 ＋ than」を使います。

 ex 4) Women are promoted <u>less</u> often than men. (Chapter 3 本文第 2 段落)

(v) ただし、little の比較級としての less や、many, much の比較級としての more もあります。

 ex 5) Women earn <u>less</u> than men, even when they do the same job. (Chapter 3 本文第 2 段落)
 ex 6) Companies should be encouraged to hire <u>more</u> people with disabilities. (本文第 5 段落)

✏ Grammar Practice

次の日本語文に合うように英語文を完成させましょう。ただし文頭に来る語も小文字にしてあります。

1. 彼の態度が状況をさらに悪化させました。

 [even / his attitude / situation / worse / the / made].

 _____

2. よりよい暮らしをしたいなら、そのために努力すべきです。

 [live / an effort / you should / if / to do so / want to / you / better, / make].

 _____

3. その会社は英語のネイティブスピーカーをもっと雇うことを決めました。

 [decided / English speakers / the company / to / native / hire/ more].

 _____

4. 屋外で過ごす子どものほうが、過ごさない子どもより健康です。

[healthier / children / who / than / spend time / who don't / those / outdoors / are].

_____

6 Dialogue 🎵 57

音声を聞いて、日本語を参考にしながら空欄に聞き取った英語を書きましょう。

Tina is talking to her friend Hiroki, a Japanese exchange student in the US, about her plans to get her dog Stirling certified as a therapy animal.

Hiroki: So Tina, _____ before Stirling gets

(どのくらいかかる)

certified as a therapy dog?

Tina: _____ , I hope. But both Stirling and I have to

(あまり長くはかからない)

pass the test.

Hiroki: What? Both of you have to take the test?

Tina: Yeah! He has to be a *good boy* and obey. I have to prove that I can

control him.

Hiroki: So, are you worried? I mean, the two of you have been training for

weeks.

Tina: I think we'll pass. Then finally we'll be able to _____

_____ . That's my goal.

(障害のある人を助ける)

Hiroki: Don't worry. Everybody's gonna love Stirling. He's the best!

Note | **certify:** 〜に資格を与える

---

7 Now It's Your Turn!

次の3つのトピックから1つ選び、回答例や Useful Expressions を参考にしながらパートナーと話し合ってみましょう。準備として、自分の意見をまとめておくと話し合いやすくなります。

1. Disability is both a medical condition and a social problem. In your opinion, which one is harder to solve?

2. Do you think that the government in Japan is doing enough to help people with disabilities live better?

3. Do you agree/disagree that volunteer work is important?

番号：

自分の意見

....

....

....

回答例

1. For me, definitely the medical condition. We've gotta have new medications and – in the future – care robots.

2. No. They've gotta do more. If you go to a subway in Japan, there're not enough ramps or elevators. I mean, it's not "user-friendly" to somebody in a wheelchair.

3. Volunteering is important because it's a great way to help people with disabilities. It's good for them, but also for us because helping others makes us feel good.

Useful Expressions

- There're not enough ...: ～が十分にない
- It's not "user-friendly" to ...: それは～に対して「利用しやすい」ものではありません。
- It's a great way to help people with disabilities.: それは、障害者の方を助けるすばらしい方法です。
- I agree, but I think that ...: 賛成ですが、私は～と考えます。

Chapter 15 *A Special Message*

本章では、著者のDr. Joan McConnellから皆さんへのメッセージを紹介しています。

「時代」は常に移り変わり、その移り変わりと共に「世界」も変わっていきます。そういった世界に生きる皆さんの将来に本書が少しでも役立つことを願っています。

1 Pre-Reading Questions 58

以下のイラストを参考にして、英文の下線部の意味を枠内の選択肢より選んで記号（a 〜 f）で答えましょう。

| 1 planets | 2 rarely | 3 rapid |
| 4 ancestors | 5 expand | 6 in your hands |

1. The earth is one of the <u>planets</u> in our solar system.　　　[　　]
2. I <u>rarely</u> see her because she lives in Hawaii.　　　[　　]
3. Change is <u>rapid</u> in our highly connected world.　　　[　　]
4. My <u>ancestors</u> came to the US from Scotland.　　　[　　]
5. Reading is an excellent way to <u>expand</u> your knowledge about the world.
　　　[　　]
6. You're the boss, so the final decision is <u>in your hands</u>.　　　[　　]

| a) 祖先 | b) あなた次第 | c) 急速な |
| d) 惑星 | e) めったに〜しない | f) 拡大する |

2 Reading Passage 🔊 59

Dear Students,

    In this final chapter, I would like to share some thoughts with you.

    Change, as you know, is a natural part of life. It affects individuals, nations, cultures, languages and even our planet. Sometimes change is

5 good, but other times it is bad. As "citizens of the world," you have the responsibility to support and encourage positive change. That's the best way to slow down – perhaps even stop – negative change.

    In the past, there were times when change happened very slowly. People lived in small, isolated communities, and rarely had contact with "outsiders."

10 Today, instead, change is extremely rapid because we live in a highly connected world. Unlike our ancestors, we have lots of contact with people from different countries and different cultures.

    If you want to understand the changes taking place today, you have to know what's going on in the world. Reading is one of the best ways to

15 expand your knowledge. With this powerful skill, you can learn about our *changing times* and *changing worlds*. Then you'll be able to support change that improves our lives and helps our planet. Perhaps you'll also be able to stop change that harms our lives and hurts our planet.

    More so than ever before, it's important to understand change and to push

20 it in a positive direction. So please learn about our *changing times*. Talk about our *changing worlds*.

    Remember that the future is in your hands!

    With my best wishes to all of you,

Dr. Joanie McConnell

(Words: 250)

isolated: 孤立した、分離した
outsiders: 部外者、外部の人間
more so than ever before: かつてないほ

どそうである、これまでよりももっと当てはまる
with my best wishes to ～: ～に幸せを
祈る気持ちを込めて、～のご多幸を祈って

❸ Comprehension Questions

本文の内容に合っている文には T を、合っていない文には F を [　] に記入しましょう。

1. As "citizens of the world," we have to support all kinds of change.

　　　　　　　　　　　　　　　　　　　　　　　　　　　　　[　　]

2. Change is slow when people live in highly connected communities.

　　　　　　　　　　　　　　　　　　　　　　　　　　　　　[　　]

3. Reading is the only powetful skill that expands your knowleage of the world.　　　　　　　　　　　　　　　　　　　　　　[　　]

4. You have to understand what's happening in the world if you want to support positive change.　　　　　　　　　　　　　　[　　]

❹ Guided Summary　🖸 60

次の英文は本文を要約したものです。(1) から (8) の空所に、下の (a) ～ (h) から適語を選んで記入し文を完成させましょう。

Change is a (1)＿＿＿＿＿ part of life. It (2)＿＿＿＿＿ individuals, nations, cultures, languages and even the (3)＿＿＿＿＿. As "citizens of the world," you have the (4)＿＿＿＿＿ to support positive change and to stop negative change. Today change is rapid in our highly (5)＿＿＿＿＿ world. To (6)＿＿＿＿＿ change, you have to know what's going on in the world. Reading is one of the best ways to learn about our *changing times* and our *changing worlds*. Remember that the (7)＿＿＿＿＿ is in your (8)＿＿＿＿＿.

🔊 Word List

(a) planet　　(b) connected　　(c) hands　　(d) responsibility

(e) natural　　(f) future　　(g) affects　　(h) understand

5 Essential Grammar

Chapter15 の文章中、下記 Chapter 1 ～ Chapter 14 までの Essential Grammar の文法内容を探し、下線を引きチャプター番号を記してみましょう。

Chapter 1: 接続詞
　◆等位接続詞　◆従位接続詞

Chapter 2: 現在形
　◆現在形の形

Chapter 3: 助動詞
　◆ can　◆ should　◆ must　◆ may

Chapter 4: 進行形
　◆現在進行形　◆過去進行形　◆現在完了　◆進行形　◆受動態の進行形（進行形の受動態）

Chapter 5: 過去形
　◆過去形の形

Chapter 6: 動名詞
　◆動名詞の働き　◆動名詞を使う頻出表現

Chapter 7: 否定文
　◆ not　◆ no　◆ not always　◆ no longer

Chapter 8: 不定詞
　◆名詞用法　◆形容詞用法　◆副詞用法

Chapter 9: 前置詞
　◆ about　◆ among　◆ as　◆ by　◆ for　◆ in　◆ of　◆ on　◆ with

Chapter 10: 現在完了形
　◆現在完了形が表す意味

Chapter 11: 使役動詞など
　◆ make　◆ let　◆ have　◆ help

Chapter 12: 受動態
　◆現在形の受動態　◆過去形の受動態　◆未来形の受動態

Chapter 13: 関係代名詞・関係副詞
　◆関係代名詞　◆関係副詞

Chapter 14: 比較
　◆比較級の作り方と注意点

✐ Grammar Practice

次の日本語文に合うように英語文を完成させましょう。ただし文頭に来る語も小文字にしてあります。

1. 彼の意見をより明確に理解したいなら、あなたは彼ともっと話すべきです。

   [understand his opinion / if you / should / with him / want to / more clearly, / talk more / you].

2. 読書は心をリラックスさせるのに最もよい方法の1つです。

   [of / relax / reading / the best ways / your mind / to / one / is].

   _____

3. あなたは問題を抱えている友だちを助けることができます。

   [a problem / help / your / has / can / who / you / friend].

   _____

4. 異なる国の人々や異なる文化の人々を理解することが重要です。

   [different countries / people from / it's / and / important / different cultures / understand / to].

   _____

6 Dialogue 🎧 61

音声を聞いて、日本語を参考にしながら空欄に聞き取った英語を書きましょう。

Joanie and Kiyoshi are talking about writing textbooks.

Kiyoshi: Joanie, you've been writing textbooks for a long time. Why?

Joanie: Because _____ to students. It lets
　　　　　　　　　　　（～に手を差し伸べるのによい方法）
me share my experiences and ideas with them.

Kiyoshi: Sorry _____, but what's your most
　　　　　　　　　（個人的なことに踏み入っていたらごめんなさい）
important message?

Joanie: _____. Remember that reading is
　　　　　　　　　（新しい考えに心を開きましょう）
one of the best ways to learn about what's going on in the world.

Kiyoshi: I agree 100 percent! Students must understand our *changing times*
and our *changing worlds* so they can support positive change.

Joanie: These students really have a big responsibility because the future is
in their hands.

🌐 **Did You Know?**

1867年、アルフレッド・ノーベル（1833-1896）は、ダイナマイトを発明しました。強力な爆薬で、建築や採鉱だけでなく、戦時中には兵器としても使用されました。彼は、「死の商人」(merchant of death) として人々に記憶されるだろうと危惧されていましたが、逆境を好転させます。彼は莫大な私財を投げ打ちノーベル賞を設立しました。現在、ノーベル賞は世界的に名誉のある平和の証となっています。

7 Now It's Your Turn!

次の３つのトピックから１つ選び、回答例や Useful Expressions を参考にしながらパートナーと話し合ってみましょう。準備として、自分の意見をまとめておくと話し合いやすくなります。

1. Change is a natural part of life. Sometimes it's good, but other times it's bad. Are you afraid of change?

2. Do you agree that reading is one of the best ways to learn about what's going on in the world?

3. Do you agree with the author that the future is in your hands?

番号：☐

自分の意見

....

....

....

回答例

1. Change may be a natural part of life, but I'm really afraid of bad change, especially climate change. I'm afraid that we may do too little too late. And then what?

2. No, I don't. I think it's better, faster and easier to *see* what's going on in the world. Pictures are more powerful than words.

3. I agree 100 percent! That's a great message. I want to support good change and stop bad change.

Useful Expressions

- I'm really afraid of ...: 私は本当に〜を恐れています。
- Reading gives you more information so you can ...: 読書はあなたにより多くの情報をもたらします。ですからあなたは〜ができるのです。
- I want to support ...: 私は〜を支持したいです。
- Her message sounds great, but ...: 彼女のメッセージは素晴らしいです。しかし〜

TEXT PRODUCTION STAFF

edited by	編集
Takashi Kudo	工藤 隆志

cover design by	表紙デザイン
Nobuyoshi Fujino	藤野 伸芳

illustrated by	イラスト
Yoko Sekine	関根 庸子

CD PRODUCTION STAFF

narrated by	吹き込み者
Dominic Allen (AmE)	ドミニク・アレン（アメリカ英語）
Ilana Labourene (AmE)	イラーナ・ラボリン（アメリカ英語）

Changing Times, Changing Worlds
やさしく読める社会事情

2020年1月20日　初版発行
2023年3月5日　第5刷発行

著　者	Joan McConnell
	山内 圭
発行者	佐野 英一郎
発行所	株式会社 成美堂

〒101-0052　東京都千代田区神田小川町3-22
TEL 03-3291-2261　FAX 03-3293-5490
https://www.seibido.co.jp

印刷・製本　　倉敷印刷株式会社

ISBN 978-4-7919-7207-4　　　　　Printed in Japan